Jesus and the T45 Option

Larry Smith

Published by Larry Smith, 2024.

While every precaution has been taken in the preparation of this book, the publisher assumes no responsibility for errors or omissions, or for damages resulting from the use of the information contained herein.

JESUS AND THE T45 OPTION

First edition. June 25, 2024.

ISBN: 979-8224137459

Written by Larry Smith.

ACKNOWLEDGEMENTS

Based on True Events

Any work attempted should begin with the acknowledgement that the worker is but a part of the finished product. The magnitude of the project holds the least importance. It is with the encouragement and support of others that a project becomes a reality.

All credit is first to the God of the Bible. "Without Him was not anything made that was made." John 1:3.

We should acknowledge others created by God for their input and encouragement.

For this small project, there is endless gratitude for my wife Gail who now resides in the Kingdom of God.

Gratefulness and appreciation is also extended to:

Linda Gobble, a true sister in Christ

Pastor Mickey Brackin

Andy Jones

This work is dedicated to these and the many workers in the ministry of the Fellowship of Christian Athletes.

Chapter One

Shadows of the Past

A gentle warmth radiated from the small flames that danced above the artificial logs in Garry's gas fireplace. He was almost mesmerized by the yellowish glow of the flames. The warmth gave him an almost supernatural sense of serenity as he sat in his favorite chair. It was a simple faded brown leather recliner. It was neither remarkable nor important to anyone else. The chair had become a personal sanctuary to his aging body. It received him as a close friend that seemed to conform itself to his needs and listened to his thoughts without interruption.

The small end table next to his chair acted as a catch-all for whatever book or article caught his attention. He lifted the coffee cup sitting on the table next to an old high school yearbook. The warmth emanating from the cup and fireplace seemed to authenticate his sense of security and peace. It was a welcomed feeling that left him unthreatened by the scene unfolding outside the window just a couple of feet from him. The changing leaves falling from the trees lining the street floated to the ground as if in a choreographed descent. They were signaling the end of a season.

"Through many dangers toils and snares, I have already come." The sound of the words from the song that had become a hallmark in Christian music, floated gently from the kitchen to the living room and landed softly on Garry's ears. Barb, his wife and soul mate for over forty years, could be heard moving about the kitchen, creating a pleasant segue for his thoughts.

Barb and Garry were like two sides of a well minted coin. Though different, the two sides of a coin complete its value. Barb had become the center of the physical world that he knew so well. More importantly, she had become his motivation and inspiration to completely surrender himself to Jesus Christ. Her voice was always sympathetic, considerate, understanding, compassionate and good natured. They were qualities that were perhaps awe-inspiring, but Garry would often find them counter to his perception of others. She was truly the other side of the coin for which he was a part.

On Garry's side of the coin was the perception that everyone wore a mask to hide their true intentions. Garry knew his perception of most people was no doubt the result of his years of experience as a criminal investigator in law enforcement. His mind was analytical. He would often scrutinize every jot and tittle of a situation before coming to a conclusion. That is, if he came to a conclusion at all. Everything for him had to be based on evidence at hand.

Comparing him to Joe Friday, the Jack Webb character in the TV series, Dragnet, Barb would often say, "Alright Joe, enough already. Sometimes it's not 'just the facts Ma'am,' you have to go with your heart!" Although Garry often disapproved of her analogy, he also knew she was most often right.

Garry took a sip of his coffee and smiled as he remembered her saying he reminded her of a story about two small boys. "One little boy," she said as she unfolded the parable, "stayed in his room with all his toys and wouldn't come out. The little boy wanted to keep all the toys to himself. He was very comfortable with them and didn't want to let them out of his sight. The boy was always sad because he couldn't decide which toy to play with. He never looked beyond what he could see right in front of him."

"The other little boy," she continued, "visited a farm for the first time. He ran straight to the barn and went in side. He ran from one stall to the next looking inside. Finally, his Dad asked what he was doing."

"With all this manure in here," shouted the boy, "there's got to be a pony somewhere."

"Which of the two boys do you think you are most like?" Barb asked Garry as her left eyebrow ascended above the other, raising the corner of her mouth into a slight smirk. It wasn't enough for the expression to reveal what she was thinking. She concluded without Garry saying a word. "That's right. We both know."

The dancing flames of the fireplace created a gentle movement of light and shadows that held Garry's deep reflective thoughts of Barb until the thoughts were interrupted by his old high school yearbook coming into focus in his peripheral vision.

Lying among the catch-all items on the table beside his chair, the little white book, now more than a half century old, appeared to be symbolic of passing time.

The soft puffiness and glimmer of the once white pseudo leather covering, and the luster of its raven black embossed letters at one time, seemed to shout the word Wildcats. The cover was now only a shroud in frail decline, with faded letters that could only whisper of past memories.

As he lifted the book slowly, showing regard for its ability to have endured the passing of time, Garry's eyes panned across familiar faces. A slight smile formed as he recognized some of his old friends who had been members of his graduating class. Occasionally, his eyes would squint as he tried to remember others.

Eventually, he turned to the picture of the varsity football team he played with fifty years earlier. Pushing his glasses firmly into place, he searched the faces of each player. He remembered most of them. Many of the faces, like his own, would now be transformed by the unavoidable and sometimes unkind process of time. As he struggled to remember some of their names, he realized that some members of the team had passed away. Garry himself was nearing seventy.

He brought his right hand to his chest and made a couple of gentle circling motions around his heart, remembering he had suffered a heart attack, by-pass surgery, and several stints being pushed into arteries leading to his heart.

He took a long deep breath, leaned back in his chair and allowed a sigh to escape. The sigh was not a response to his present physical condition. It was from remembering his dream to play football from the age of six. It was the unremitting disappointment, inability, and long-suffering during his first three years of high school, just trying to be part of the team. It was the unique interrelationship with his football experience and his Christian walk. It was the significance of five plays from the T formation offense that symbolized the experiences.

"Why the solemn expression?" Barb asked as she entered the room with fresh coffee. Garry remained silent for several seconds, then released another sigh. Barb began pouring the coffee, sharing quick glances between the cup and Garry as she waited for his answer. "Well, don't go away. I'll be right back. This looks somewhat serious." She said as she slightly pursed her lips and tilted her head to one side. Smiling to herself as she walked away, she spoke in a less audible voice but with enough amplification for Garry to hear. "My yearbook never caused me to become catatonic."

Barb returned the pot of coffee to its staging area on the coffee maker then gave the pot strict orders. "You stay at your post until I return. I'm sure you'll be called out again." She saluted the coffeepot and turned to find Garry standing in the doorway to the kitchen. His arms were folded in front of his chest. His head was cocked to one side, and his upper lip was slightly elevated at one corner. Garry's intimidating posture was undeniably erroneous. He followed with an even more erroneous attempt at imitating the voice of John Wayne. "Don't give up your day job little lady. You'll never be a comedian." Garry said as he walked toward Barb with the characteristic John Wayne stride.

"Well, looks like we both need to stay out of show business." Barb said, returning his comment with a slight chuckle. She took Garry by the arm spinning him around as she led him back to his chair. "Sit down." She said, giving her best impression of Paul Harvey. "I want to hear the 'rest of the story'".

Garry eased himself back into his chair, shifting and twisting slightly to ensure proper positioning. Barb and Garry's chairs were matching recliners separated by the catch-all table. The hum from the small electric motor that moved Barb's chair into position was a signal to Garry that she was ready to hear what he had to say.

"So, what is it about the yearbook that has you thinking so intently?" She asked."

"Well, I guess it would be a long story and you've heard part of it in a roundabout way." He said, still not looking at her."

"If you haven't noticed," she said, turning both palms up and moving her hands to the side as she looked around the room. "We're both retired. So, that means we've got time."

"Well," said Garry, "You know how your mind jumps from one thing and then another. I was looking at the picture of the team. There was Coach Hank, Jimbo, Carl, Randy and...." Garry paused for several seconds before continuing, "and of course Barry." He paused again. Barb didn't say a word. Barry was Garry's younger brother. She knew his story and was sure Garry would reveal his thoughts at the proper time.

"Anyway," Garry continued, "seeing Randy reminded me of a series of plays I ran during a game one night. The more I thought about it, the more that series of plays seemed to tell a story." Garry raised both hands above his head. "I don't know where to start." He said, showing a minor frustration.

"Why don't you start from the beginning?" Barb's coaxing brought another sigh from Garry.

"To me," he said, pulling his thoughts into focus, "Both my football experience and my Christian experience seemed to begin with a calling."

Chapter Two

The First Calling

"What do you mean by calling?" she asked. Garry smiled as she spoke the word. He was well aware that the word 'calling' had a special place in Southern Baptist vocabulary. Regardless of the variety of uses for the word, it was at the top of the hierarchy for her. Clearly it indicated a heavenly summons to serve God in some special way.

Although they had spent more than four decades together, their childhood and teen years had been spent in very different environments. She had not met Garry until he had finished his tour in the military and was into his third year of college. She was an only child and her parents were avid church goers. Garry on the other hand, had four younger brothers, and his parents never attended church with him. Garry held a long pause considering how his first calling came about. At least he considered it to be his first calling. It was to play football.

As Garry began to explain, his thoughts carried him back to the first grade and the small elementary school he had attended in 1954. The L shaped, split-level, red brick building was only three years old at the time Garry started school. It was also the most modern building in the small rural county of about twelve thousand people.

The lower part of the L shaped building consisted of two floors. The lower floor was nestled into a rolling embankment and housed first and second graders. The elongated portion of the L lay along the top of the embankment and had only one floor for third through sixth graders.

The elementary school's more modern design created only a slight contrast to the high school which was constructed in the 1930s. It was connected to the elementary school by a covered walkway.

The high school, a two story building accented by a square shaped three story tower near the end opposite the elementary school, had been a crowning achievement for the county at the time of its construction. Combined, they were symbolic of the educational ascent to growth and prosperity.

Still holding the yearbook, Garry's eyes focused on Coach Hank. He closed his eyes and visualized the only part of his football experience that he cherished. That was his senior year. But, it was in the first grade that the first calling became apparent.

Although Garry's mother tried to prepare him for the first grade experience, it was still somewhat of a culture shock to be around so many people at one time. There were probably as many as three hundred people in both schools. When the social life of a six year old consisted of a few cousins, two sets of aunts and uncles and grand parents, three hundred kids in one place was a spectacle to behold.

That first year in school was also the first time Garry ever saw a football player in full uniform. Since Garry's family didn't get a TV until his second grade year, he had never even seen a ball game. On one very nice autumn afternoon, his first grade teacher, Mrs. Shirley, took the class to watch the team practice.

As if she had been a female version of the pied piper in the story she had read to the class a few days earlier, the little class of about thirty first graders followed Mrs. Shirley across the play ground. As they crossed the play ground, a chorus of deep booming voices could be heard in the distance.

Over and over the sound reverberated, rising from beneath the earth and soaring into the autumn sky above. "Hut, two, three, four," came the hidden and booming deep voices contrasting the cheerful voices of the group of first graders as they marched forward in the direction of the strange sound. Garry had never heard anything like it.

The practice field for the high school football team was a low lying field at the bottom of a steep slope about forty or fifty feet below the rim that created a separation from the elementary play ground.

The almost menacing cadence from the team grew with each step the class took. They approached the edge of the playground that would be their vantage point. The field below opened to them as if they were peering into an active volcano. What a sight!

Garry's eyes instantly sprang to full wide at what was before him. These were people alright and all boys he was sure. But they were big boys! He found himself mesmerized by the player's helmets and the size of their shoulders. The uniforms made them look superhuman.

They were lined up about eight wide and four deep. A man wearing a cap and holding a whistle in his mouth was standing in front of all the others. Garry was smart enough to know that the man wearing the cap and whistle was the most important one of all. Seven years later, Garry would have the opportunity to be part of the team led by coach Hank.

Garry couldn't take his eyes of the players on the field. With each count, they would swing their feet apart and throw their hands over their heads. Mrs. Shirley informed the class that the exercise they were doing was called jumping jacks. Garry turned to his best friend Joe for answers. He knew Joe would have them.

Joe became Garry's best friend not only because he had the same last name, but because he was the first one to talk to Garry when he started school. Joe was not a country boy like Garry. He actually lived in the city limits in a town of more than 2,000 people. Garry quickly learned Joe was sophisticated.

"What's on their feet?" Garry asked, his eyes narrowing indicating puzzlement.

"They're football shoes." Joe responded with a look that quickly morphed from confusion to disbelief.

"But look on the bottoms." Garry said excitedly.

"Well yeah." Joe said as his eyes widened in more disbelief at such ignorance. His head pressed forward accenting each word, reminding Garry of one of the chickens as it walked across the back yard at his house. He would chuckle as their heads pressed forward in time with each step. "They're steel cleats!" Joe's remark resonated with a tone that seemed to mock Garry's ignorance.

"Why would they have steel spikes on the bottom of their shoes?" Garry asked in amazement.

Joe responded with an air of superior knowledge. After all, he had seen a real high school football game in person. "They keep your feet from sliding out from under you when you run and boy they sure can dig into you if you get stepped on!" Joe said crossing his arms with pride. Garry stared at him momentarily impressed with his knowledge and amused at the fact that Joe reminded him so much of the image painted on the side of his lunch box. The image was the TV puppet Howdy Doody.

Garry watched with undivided attention as some of the players broke from their formation and formed a single line facing the opposite end of the field. The player who had been leading the exercises shouted, "Down!" and a player in front of him bent forward and placed his hands on the ball. The first player in the line bent down with one elbow on his knee and the other hand on the ground. Garry thought he looked like a three legged dog.

The player in charge placed his hands against the backside of the one who was touching the football. Garry tilted his head to one side as a questioning look developed on his face. He looked at Joe but decided it would be better not to ask another question.

The player holding the ball on the ground quickly placed the ball in the other player's hands who then quickly started running backwards holding the ball with both hands up near his face. He watched the other three legged dog player who had been at the front of the line run forward several steps, quickly turn his head and shoulders as if he was going to run to the left, then dart back to the right.

The player with the ball threw it as the other player was running. The player caught the ball in full stride and rolled on the ground and bounced to his feet as if he had rolled across a soft mattress. Garry noticed Mrs. Shirley looking at him smiling as he shouted, "Wow!"

The man with the whistle blew a quick tweet and shouted something Garry couldn't understand. The players split into two separate groups and faced each other in a single file. One player bent over into the three legged dog position while the other player remained standing looking at the man with the whistle. The man with the whistle tossed him the ball and the two players crashed together. The sound of the collision brought Garry to his feet again as the two players fell to the ground. They just as quickly jumped to their feet and went to the back of their respective lines.

"That had to hurt bad!" Garry said as Joe stood up beside him. "Naw," Joe said almost in a yawn. They got pads on. They don't feel nothin." "Wow!" Garry exclaimed again almost in a whisper.

"Let's go class. Mrs. Shirley called out. It's time to go back in." Garry absolutely did not want to leave. He was hooked. He knew he wanted to play football. It most likely wasn't the Holy Spirit speaking to him, but he was sure he heard the call.

Chapter Three

The Second Calling

The Christian experience began when Garry was nine. Mr. Andy, as he was called by all the kids who got to know him, stopped to visit one summer morning to invite Garry's family to church. Garry was completely unaware at the time that his parents were charter members of the church Mr. Andy was inviting them to attend.

He only learned about their involvement decades later. Garry had faint memories of being in church a few times when he was only three or four. He would learn later why his parents stopped going and didn't talk about it.

While Mr. Andy was talking, Garry clearly felt the desire to go to church, but his mother passed Mr. Andy off with, "Well, I don't know. We'll see." Without hesitation, Garry blurted out, "I want to go." Mr. Andy said he drove the church bus and would be glad to stop and give Garry and his brothers a ride on Sunday morning. Although both his brothers would decline, Garry told Mr. Andy he would be ready.

He couldn't understand it, but Sunday morning found Garry excited about a new adventure as the 1956 panel wagon that had been transformed into a church bus stopped in front of the house. Garry was the first passenger on the bus giving Mr. Andy an opportunity to discuss the Sunday School class he was teaching and to invite Garry to attend.

The encounter with Mr. Andy gave Garry the opportunity to develop a special respect for the man who would become his Christian role model for years to come. Garry rode the bus every Sunday morning and evening until he was old enough to drive the family car himself. His parents never attended church with him. In fact, Garry was the only one in his family who ever went to church.

The large red brick building with its stained glass windows in front of him seemed to dissolve into the small white church a few miles away. It was the Church from which this one had sprung.

More like a grand American Eagle than a church, that small pure white clapboard structure from the past, sat resolute at the summit of a large hill overlooking the two-lane highway below as if to say to the passersby, "Here I am. You should come for a closer look. You'll like what you see." He remembered being mesmerized as he sat in one of a half dozen classrooms in the rear of the little church listening to Mr. Andy talk about the wonderful promises of the gospel.

The new church where the congregation now met was an almost exaggerated contrast to the old church that now sat abandoned and beginning to fade from lack of attention. After finally deciding to enter the new building, Garry felt a strange resistance. The service was already in progress. Before opening one of the large wooden doors that led from the foyer to the sanctuary, he peered through one of the small diamond shaped window that was placed at eye level allowing the one entering to see what was going on inside.

The Pastor was walking toward the Pulpit to welcome everyone. Johnny was standing in front of the choir getting ready to lead the first song as he had done since the first time Garry saw him. Mr. Andy was sitting with his family in his regular pew at the front on the right side of the sanctuary.

Garry recalled a bible verse he had heard in Sunday School. It was, "They draw close to me with their words, but there hearts are far from me."

He knew those words certainly didn't describe everyone, but he had seen enough in the few short years that he had attended church, that they applied to many.

In 1964, there had been a lot of talk about integration. He remembered hearing a man speaking to others in the church saying, "They have their place and we have ours." Although he had attended the church for only a few years, he had heard enough church discussion to realize the statement didn't apply to race alone. On more than one occasion, he had heard some who were supposed to be leaders in the church discuss how many churches were falling short of the gospel because of their particular beliefs. They also had their place, but it was with their own denomination and not the one Garry was attending.

Garry stood alone, looking through the small window for what seemed like several minutes, then whispered to himself, "Something is missing." Surely Heaven wasn't segregated or broken into denominations." Garry cracked the door slightly. His intention was to enter. Pausing for a few seconds, he closed the door. He walked out and never went back. He just quit going to church as abruptly as he had started.

Chapter Four

Change

Barb's gentle touch on Garry's shoulder interrupted his thoughts. "Come back to earth and get on with your story," she said. Garry knew he often bounced from one thought to the next, often covering decades and vast distances.

A sigh slipped from Garry's lips along with a low whisper, "Well, this old body is about used up, but I can still see Coach Hank standing on the sidelines. Garry chuckled and said, I can still hear him calling me."

"Guy-ri!" Coach Hank called from the sidelines. "Come heah son." He never pronounced the name correctly. Even with the extra r instead of the one r that is normally used to spell the name. Garry seemed like such a simple name to pronounce. However, Garry knew that when Coach Hank called the quarterback to the sidelines instead of sending a play in with a substitute, he wanted something special to happen. The team was ahead 21 to nothing at the start of the third quarter and Coach Hank's comments were all positive during the halftime pep talk.

As he jogged to the sideline, Garry tried to second guess what Coach Hank had in mind, knowing all the time that trying to second guess Coach Hank was a waste of mental energy. "Surely he's not displeased with the way the game was going." Garry thought to himself. "It must be me." Garry had a lifelong habit of seeing himself as never meeting expectations.

With his left foot forward, his leg straight, and shoulders tilted forward, Coach Hank stood with both arms folded across his chest as if an invisible force circled his waist, preventing him from stepping onto the field. His lower jaw pressing down, first on one side then the other as his teeth purposefully manipulated the piece of Wrigley's gum in his mouth, giving the impression that his face was walking because his feet couldn't. The overall countenance was clear. He wanted to make a change. Garry was not ready for his instruction.

As Garry reached the sideline, Coach Hank placed his hand on Garry's shoulder pad and leaned close. The gentle shake of the shoulder pad by Coach Hank was a message in itself that seemed to say, "I know you'll understand." But it was the spoken words that were unmistakable.

"I want you to run Randy a lot." Garry didn't answer and hoped his face revealed the lack of expression that said, "Sure coach. Whatever you say." Garry only nodded and ran back to the huddle.

The glow from the lights flooding the small country stadium seemed less luminous as Garry returned to the field. As his cleats dug into the turf that was becoming moist with dew, his mind was being saturated with thoughts. None of them were positive. Garry's dissatisfaction with the coach's request was quickly turning to anger and frustration. A change was underway.

Change, whether microscopic or catastrophic, is still change. The course of a ship at sea altered by the slightest movement of the rudder or constant nudging of a mighty wind is altered and the final destination is no longer the same. Garry knew his attitude had changed. He also knew he didn't want the team to see the spirit that was taking charge of his thoughts, but the sound and words from Coach Hank's voice had its effect.

From the origin of the sound that creates the motion of the waves that touch and activate the receptacle inside the ear, the waves travel to three tiny bones that increase the vibration and send them further along their way to an area of fluid. The fluid ripples as the waves move along, putting hair cells into motion like cattails at the edge of a pond. The hair cells, like well choreographed dancers responding to waves of music, tilt to one side then open to receive special chemicals that rush in, creating an electrical signal.

The signal reaches its final destination-that most mysterious of all human organs-the brain. The result is sound with meaning. Garry would recall these events years later and think how marvelous is the human design! He would also remember the sound, "Run Randy."

As the wind and rudder effect the direction of a ship, catastrophic events or simple spoken words can likewise alter a course upon which the mind is set. Words that began as nothing more than unintelligible sounds forming unseen waves passing through intangible space like ripples over a pond touching gently against a distant shore, touched that portion of Garry's ear that transforms them into clear and concise meaning.

Meaning is a matter of interpretation that is filtered through years of countless events that must be prioritized and acted upon. The outcome is the formulation of an emotion that is translated into action, followed by consequence. The consequence hinges on just one thing-choice.

The change that was about to take place in the game would be much more than Garry could have imagined. Little did he know that the next series of plays he was about to call would mirror his Christian walk for the next several decades.

The usual sights and sounds of a Friday night high school football game faded with the encroachment of recent memories. This was his senior year in high school. Garry had wanted to play football since the first grade. All he could think about was what had transpired in the nearly four years since he finally had the chance to actually play. Garry did not doubt that his high school football career had been the most humiliating, frustrating, embarrassing, discouraging and failure filled experience he would probably ever have. Now the coach wanted him to run Randy. Yes in deed, change was coming!

Garry had nothing against Randy. He only met him for the first time in his senior year. Randy was a sophomore who transferred from an even smaller country school that was forced to shut down, as had several others like it. The days of the little white one room country schoolhouse had gone the way of the Studebaker and Edsel. They had become symbols of the changing times.

Obviously, Randy had all the qualifications of an athlete that were seriously lacking for Garry, except for one. Randy had never played football on a real team before. Randy's well chiseled body and the fact that he was at least 6 inches taller than Garry revealed superior athletic ability. It probably gave him the ability to run twice as fast, but Garry noticed him running plays during practice and he appeared somewhat awkward, as if his mind couldn't get his muscles to cooperate completely.

Having only a few weeks to learn plays also created a handicap. He would get confused on which way to go when the ball was snapped. But Randy appeared eager to learn. He usually was quiet but amicable. His demeanor projected insecurity, highlighted by his being associated mostly with a friend of his who transferred from the same school.

Garry would look back over the fifty years that would pass since that night, and realize how closely his high school football career mirrored his Christian experience-an experience that was most humiliating, frustrating, embarrassing, discouraging and filled with failure. In his mind, his Christian career, like his football career, closely resembled each other in that his dream was to one day cross the goal line for his own touchdown instead of passing the opportunity off to someone else. If football was an example, the outlook was not so good.

Chapter Five

The Authority

Garry knew his choice was to obey or not to obey. Randy took his position at the center in the second line of the huddle. The linemen, facing the opposing team about twenty yards away, positioned themselves three each to the left and right of Carl the center. Randy, the fullback, stood behind Carl with the right and left halfback on each side of him. Randy had replaced George, The first team full back. The two were a stark contrast.

Though formidable would be an understatement in describing George's size, it would not be his size that Garry would always remember. It would be the memory of spring practice a year and a half earlier, when he brought that six three, two hundred fifty pound monstrosity he referred to as a body, crashing through the center of the line and headed full steam for the right defensive halfback. That defensive halfback was a five eleven, 125 pound Garry. Garry was ending his sophomore year and, for the first time, got to be involved in scrimmage.

More like a prehistoric monster in a bad Japanese movie than a high school football player, George towered above other players on the team. The unfortunate second team players who were chosen to scrimmage against George often met the same fate as the tall buildings of Tokyo that were crushed down by the mighty Godzilla.

The correct strategy for a tackle would be for Garry to hit George low and trip him up. Before he could make his move, George was already in the secondary. The middle linebacker made the mistake of grasping George's shoulders. He was soon just along for the ride. Garry assisted as best he could and hit George at the waist. Garry was not sure George even knew he was there. George was still moving forward when the corner linebacker dove at his ankles, taking both of George's feet from under him. Garry hit the ground first, landing flat on his back. It couldn't have taken more than a couple of seconds for fulfillment of the inevitable.

Garry looked up from the ground to see a dark ominous cloud obliterating the sun and all the heavens. Before the cloud, there was fresh new spring grass moving with the gentle breeze. The air was clean with the smell of honeysuckles. But now, the cloud was descending from an unhappy sky. An unforgiving storm was about to descend with a vengeance upon Garry.

When George's feet were taken from beneath him, 250 pounds went into a free fall. Garry's chest broke the fall when George's enormous butt landed on it. The air that was left in Garry's lungs exploded from his mouth and nose. It felt as if his sternum touched his spine. Garry made no sound. He couldn't. There was no air to move the vocal chords. Garry couldn't be sure he still had vocal chords. For all he knew, they left his body with the air that was so rapidly forced out.

Garry could hear Coach Hank say, "Good Lawd! George fell on 'im!" Garry could see the coach kneeling beside him. "Guy-ri, can you breathe son?" He asked. Garry could only shake his head. When he finally caught his breath, Coach Hank sent him to the hospital for a checkup. The only thing injured was Garry's pride. The next day, he was back at practice.

Now here he was a year and a half later as quarterback, looking at George's replacement for the next few plays. Randy's expression was one of anticipation and uncertainty. Garry was certain his own expression revealed uncertainty as well. Each member of the team was also looking at both Randy and Garry with anticipation. They knew the call would involve Randy, but probably thought no

more of the situation than what the play call might be. From the time Coach Hank said, "Run Randy," Garry's mind had been churning. Here was a guy who had only been on the team for a few weeks. Garry felt certain he understood Coach Hank's plan, and he didn't like it at all.

Garry had waited eight years to be on the football team. He spent his first two years doing every exercise, running every lap, and doing every drill other team members had done. But there is one thing he didn't do, and that was play. In fact, Garry's entire freshman and sophomore years ended without him being in one play during a game. How humiliating it had been to know that when the team was a couple of touchdowns ahead with only a few seconds left, the coach would send every Freshman in so they could at least say they had been in during an actual game. That is, every freshman except one.

Garry thought to himself, "During that whole time, I was not in on one play during practice let a lone an actual game. Now, Coach Hank wants me to run a guy who only came to this school this year. This is the first time he has ever actually been involved with a real team. He only understands the very basics of an offensive play!"

How Garry wanted to object to what Coach Hank asked him to do! So what if Randy was six inches taller and weighed 60 pounds more. So what if he could run twice as fast as Garry. Garry was the quarterback. He had earned his position. "Okay", he admitted to himself, "Maybe I sort of earned it."

"I want you all to know that pride comes before a fall." Although Garry had not been to church in several months, Mr. Andy's words pranced into his mind with the sound of the band's rendition of the all too familiar tune, Our Boys Gonna Shine Tonight.

Mr. Andy certainly had a profound effect on him during those years in his Sunday school class. He had been a star basketball player in the small neighboring town during the 30s. Garry knew he could never forget the story Mr. Andy told about driving to the goal during a game as an opposing player dashed in front of him and tried to steal the ball. Mr. Andy, in mid dribble, rolled the ball over in his hand, brought it behind his back and tossed it over his left shoulder toward the basket. It went in!

Even now, Garry could imagine the smile on Mr. Andy's face as he recalled the incident. Had anyone else seen the smile, they most likely would have thought it to be pride, but anyone who had sat in Mr. Andy's Sunday school class through even one of his lessons would have discarded any such misconception. "Pride in yourself," he would say, "and being pleased with yourself are really two different things."

"One can be good: the other not so much. When you have pride in yourself, you're filling yourself with a false sense of accomplishment. But more importantly, you're giving yourself credit for whatever accomplishment you might have made. Being pleased is feeling joy for something you have done and realizing it was God who made it possible for you. The person who understands that will most often say I'm grateful, instead of look at what I have done."

Garry would remember a lot about Mr. Andy. It was like the time in the old church when Garry was 11 years old. Mr. Andy placed what at the time seemed like giant hands around both Garry's upper arms and lifted him high over his head, saying, "Garry, I'm forty eight years old today." Garry was not only impressed with Mr. Andy's teaching and sports ability, he was also amazed at how old he was and still able to play basketball.

It was Mr. Andy who first got Garry involved in sports. He organized the first Royal Ambassador group in the county. Boys between nine years old and twelve were in the organization. He obviously saw something in Garry that Garry didn't see in himself because he made Garry the first Ambassador in Chief. When he finally had enough teenage boys to form an older group, he let Garry be over them until he found a leader.

But it was his involvement with the RA basketball team that elevated Garry's appreciation for him as much as anything. He gave up his Saturday mornings to take the RA boys to the old high school gym.

It was there Garry learned about sportsmanship and teamwork. Mr. Andy could turn basketball practice into a Sunday School lesson. What was most important to Garry at the time was the fact that Mr. Andy let him play basketball and was not concerned with the fact that he was the smallest one in the group.

As he taught Garry how to make a free throw shot, it didn't matter that Garry didn't have enough strength to get the ball from the free throw line to the goal. Even after he had entered the seventh grade, Garry could not make a free shot with a two handed push. He had to throw the ball through the hoop from the foul line like he was throwing a baseball. He was just that small. Mr. Andy would quote Proverbs 23:7, "for as he thinks in his heart, so is he."

That was a quote Garry needed to remember daily. Other students would constantly remind him how small he was for his age. Even the shortest girl in his class often reminded him she was taller than he was.

"Proverbs 23:7 is a great verse," Mr. Andy would say, "but when you are too much in the world mentally, you only see what's going on around you. You focus too much on what you think is real instead of what really could be." A quote used many times reminded Garry of what Mr. Andy was eluding to. "If you're a fish, you don't know you're wet." Change can come slow, but it can come.

"Go Wildcats!" The shouts from the cheerleaders followed by the shouts from the crowd brought Garry back to the game. He leaned to the left side of the huddle saying, "T40 on 2." Then leaning to the right side repeatring, "T40 on 2." The "T" formation had been around for a while and was just about to go out of style in 1965. But it was a simple formation and easy to learn. It was one of the first things Coach Hank taught the new freshmen.

The team broke and hustled to the line of scrimmage. As he glanced at the defensive lineup, Garry followed Carl, the center to where the umpire placed the ball. They were on the 20 yard line with 80 more yards to the goal line. He knew the defensive secondary would shift as soon as he barked the word "down."

He took his position behind Carl and flipped the towel that had been dangling from the back of Carl's pants onto his back. Garry thought he probably should have dried his hands before taking the snap, but his mind centered on two things. He would keep the promise he had made to himself and never fumble the ball on the center's snap. Also, he would make sure the runner got the hand off. He didn't ask Randy in the huddle if he knew the play. It was as simple as could be.

Garry inserted the mouthpiece that was connected to his chinstrap. "Down!" The thickness of the mouthpiece made the word sound more like hound than down. Regardless of the pronunciation, both teams were listening only to the cadence. Garry was sure the defense had already heard about the quarterback they were facing. Passing the football was not his specialty. Although there was plenty of space between them and the goal line, the defensive secondary had moved forward, anticipating another run. Why not? That was what they had seen from him all night.

A defensive linebacker poised himself a couple of feet in front of Carl. Both hands stretched slightly forward, ready for the snap. Carl's hand secured the football as he waited for the next sound coming from Garry. "Set!" Garry could almost sense the tension of each of the linemen as they waited for the sound that would signal the clash.

The success of the play mostly depended on Carl moving the middle linebacker, and Randy, the right guard, moving the man in front of him. Interestingly enough, Randy the right guard and Randy, the fullback, had the same first and last names. That's where the similarities ended. Both Randys were often intentionally mistaken for the other because of their names.

Although Randy, the fullback, was new to the position and the game in general, his job was relatively simple. He had learned the "holes." The zero hole is the space between the center and right guard.

The space between the right guard and right tackle is 2. The space between the right tackle and the right end is 4. Anything beyond the right end would be 6. The holes on the left side of the line are numbered 1, 3, and 5. How simple could that be?

A T formation is a T shaped offense beginning with the line and the quarterback positioned directly behind the center. The right halfback is a little farther back and lined up between the right guard and right tackle. The left halfback is on the left side at the same distance behind the line and lined up between the left guard and left tackle. The fullback is directly behind the quarterback.

The quarter back's number is one. The right half is two, the left half is three, and the fullback is four. Randy needed only to run straight forward, take the ball from Garry, break through the zero hole and pick up some yardage. How simple could the T formation be?

When Coach Hank said, "Run Randy a lot," that was all he said. On his way back to the huddle, Garry had already decided how it would go. Randy was going to earn every inch he got. Garry thought he was being fare with Randy. Though it had crossed his mind to run a series of complicated plays, he realized Randy probably didn't know all the plays, so the T formation was ready-made for him.

Garry had learned a lot from Mr. Andy. He had taught him to respect authority. "If you can't respect proper authority on earth," he would say, "Do you really think you would respect the authority of your father in heaven?"

The truth is Coach Hank was the authority for the football team and Garry did respect him. Coach Hank had gently tried to encourage Garry to give up football and become one of the team managers which interpreted meant team gofer. The manager would gofer what ever a player wanted and bring it to him. Garry informed coach Hank he wanted to play football. Coach Hank never mentioned it again. Garry would honor the coach's authority and run Randy. He would run him a lot. But, he would run him up the middle.

Chapter Six

Spiritual Warfare

"Hut one!" Like bird dogs on the point, each lineman was motionless, waiting for the signal to retrieve. Like the huntsman with his gun cocked, they were ready for the next sound Garry made.

"Hut two!" That sound created an eruption of almost simultaneous sounds as Carl slapped the football firmly into Garry's hands. People in the stands could hear the helmets and shoulder pads crashing together to the accompaniment of grunts, groans, and the crunching of steel cleats digging into the turf. That sound is amplified many times for those in the middle of it all. The sound alone can be very intimidating.

Garry had watched Randy since he started practicing with the team. He was impressive and not afraid to hit or be hit. He had played a lot of pasture football, but this season was his first exposure to actual drill and discipline. Garry was still not too happy with the fact that it had become his job to show Randy off. At least that was his perception of Coach Hank's instructions.

Garry realized his job was simple. He just needed to make sure he held on to the football, make a slight turn to the right as Randy rushed straight forward through the zero hole, and give him the ball.

Carl and the other Randy had already made the hole a little wider by moving two defensive players back and apart. The right halfback headed for the right corner defensive linebacker. Randy shot forward like an oversized cannon ball straight into the hole. He positioned his arms perfectly for the handoff. Garry slapped the football between Randy's arms and left it with him, then faked a handoff to the left halfback as he made a pretend run around the right end. Garry followed a little wider to the outside.

Not one defensive player seemed to be pulled in by the fake run by Garry and the left halfback. They closed toward the middle after Randy.

What they encountered seemed to be more than they expected. Randy picked up about a yard after the middle linebacker slid away from Carl and hit Randy just below the shoulders. That was a big mistake! Randy was like a bull out of the gate at a rodeo.

The linebacker, with a vice like grip, held on to Randy, but he looked like a bull rider that had just been thrown with his hand still connected to the bull rope. Randy didn't go down even when the right corner linebacker joined in, followed by both defensive half backs. Randy had picked up seven yards before he was taken down. He had also moved the ball closer to the center of the field.

Randy, at 6 feet 2 inches and 185 pounds, was certainly no behemoth like George. While George was huge, for a high school football player, he wasn't the perfect image of an athlete. His usual slight smile made him appear more jovial than the wrecking ball he was. His return to the huddle was always slow paced with his right hand on his side, as if it helped him walk.

Garry watched as Randy quickly sprang to his feet once the pile of defensive players removed themselves from his back. Randy jogged back to the huddle with his fists closed as his arms pumped to the side like drivers on a locomotive. His shoulders forward, his head erect.

Randy took his place in the huddle without saying a word. He stood looking at Garry, eyes wide, as if to say, "Is that what you wanted? He appeared to be breathing the same as when the huddle broke for his first play.

That was Randy's first run in a ball game. "I had to wait until my third year in high school before I even got in a game," Garry said to himself. He could feel an unpleasant emotion beginning to churn from deep within. "Every practice session and every game found me sitting on the sidelines. I don't have time for this he thought.

We still have a game and I have crazy thoughts flashing through my mind." But the thoughts wouldn't go away. All Garry could think about was the rough rode He had been on just to get to this place and now this new guy strolls up and takes a place as if it had been his all along.

Also true was the fact that Garry was pleased to see what Randy had accomplished. Jealousy, anger, pride, contempt, resentment, selfishness, and a host of other emotions were racing through his mind. He couldn't understand why.

"For we wrestle not against flesh and blood, but against principalities, against powers, against the rulers of the darkness of this world, against spiritual wickedness in high places." Although he was speaking to a small group of Sunday School Students that ranged in ages from ten to twelve, Mr. Andy's delivery couldn't have been more sincere or purposeful if he had been talking to a large audience of adults. He was the main reason Garry attended church so regularly during those early years.

Garry was only ten years old, but Mr. Andy helped him to see there was more to life than he had previously thought. In fact, Mr. Andy's teaching helped Garry to believe there was a world other than the one he could see around him. It was a world filled with real beings that could influence him just as much as the people who were visible all around him.

It would be many years before Garry could understand that spiritual warfare was indeed real. He had actually been a casualty of the warfare during those uneventful years of football. He was also a casualty the morning he looked into the sanctuary and walked out of the church, never to return. In his early 20s, Garry would join another church. After fifteen years of being in that church, he would quit again.

But Mr. Andy's words, "as he believes in his heart, so is he," never left him. However, for many years, they worked the opposite of the way they were intended. With football, he believed what others had told him. He was too small, too slow, and too weak to be anything other than a spectator of the game in which he wanted so much to be a part of.

One Friday night during his sophomore year, after everyone on the team had played but Garry, he once again became a casualty to spiritual warfare. He took his shoes, which were the only part of the uniform that was his, and left the locker room. As he was leaving, Jimbo stopped him in the parking lot.

"Are you quitin?" Jimbo asked.

"After two years of not even being allowed to scrimmage or even get in on one play in a game, you bet I quit." Garry said half way expecting Jimbo to understand and try to talk him out of leaving the team. Jimbo's response was only one word. "Good."

Jimbo was a classmate and seemed to be the only one on the team who showed any interest in Garry the whole time he had been with the team. Jimbo had played since he was a freshman and lettered as a sophomore. Still, he wouldn't show sympathy for a quitter. At that moment, Garry could not have cared less. Enough is enough.

Walking away without looking back, Garry stopped short of his car and looked toward the ball field. The field was now dark and vacant. There were only a few cars left in the parking lot. Most of them belonged to players who were still in the locker room. The shoes that were draped across Garry's shoulders slipped and fell to the ground, scraping his right knee on the descent.

"That figures," Garry whispered to himself, "These cold hard cleats are just like the cold hard facts. You don't have what it takes. So why put yourself through this?" Garry considered his thoughts to be accurately describing his situation. Many times since then, thoughts of defeat, humiliation, and a lack of worthiness would cross his mind. It seemed to always happen as he was being confronted about some difficult situation. If he tried to discuss the situation with anyone, he would interpret their response as similar to the response he had received from Jimbo. Who cares?

Garry didn't understand it at the time, but the spiritual warfare Mr. Andy had talked about was raging full force in his mind. He was so wrapped up in disappointment that he didn't realize the thoughts were being fired into his mind by the enemy.

"You're making the right decision. You don't have to put up with this. Did you really expect Jimbo or anyone else to care if you quit? Do you think anyone cares what you do? Have your parents even been to one game? And why do you think? Because nobody cares and you don't have what it takes. That's why." He was loosing the battle and becoming a casualty of the war.

Staying in church had become even more difficult than staying with football. The reasons were much different, but the feeling of defeat was very much the same. Garry only quit football once before going back. He would quit church twice. Each time he left the church, he felt he had spent so many years wasting his time. After all the work and all the study, he saw no personal growth.

As a boy under the guidance of Mr. Andy, he had become very active and even held positions as a young boy that he would always appreciate. In fact, it was from those appointed positions, that Garry gained some sense of self esteem. But it seemed like the more dedicated he became, the less accomplished he would feel. Like football, what he learned seemed to clash with the realities of life.

Not unlike most young boys, Garry was very impressionable. But in his middle teens, it seemed that prayers weren't answered. His parents had still not attended church. He was still far from being the athlete he had prayed to become. Then there was another dose of reality. While still a teen, he watched one of the leaders of his boyhood church get into a fight with his wife in the parking lot because he had been unfaithful to her. He had respected both of them a great deal. Their wedding was the first one he had ever attended.

Garry often compared events in his life as looking into a kaleidoscope. They were always clashing. He remembered the morning he stood at the door of the sanctuary of his boyhood church. The enemy was firing at him fast and furious. "Look at those people. Do you really think they are sincere about what they believe? If they were, do you think you would have seen them do the things you have seen? Remember what you had heard about one preacher?

His view of success in the church was the size of the offering each week. You heard that from relatives and church members. Surely they knew what they were talking about. Everybody is looking out for themselves. Look at that man and woman in front of the church. You were told that the only reason they come to church was to look important. Even you can see that is true."

Failure to return to church did not lead to spiraling out of control as often is the case with teenagers. Garry had seen plenty of alcohol abuse from family and relatives while he was growing up. That was one area the attacking spirits would have no influence on him, but judging others for their behaviors or their choices was another thing all together.

"Be not conformed to this world, but be ye transformed by the renewing of the mind." Like so many parts of scripture, those words seemed to return from time to time, but would not resonate until many years later. However without knowing why, Garry was fascinated by the mind and wanted to learn how it worked. Even as a teenager, he found himself often amazed at the way people conducted themselves. After four years in the Air Force, he would have the opportunity with the GI Bill to pursue a degree in Psychology and Sociology.

It was while working on a master's degree in counseling that he decided too much theory was being taught as absolutes for defining human behavior. It seemed to work for most students, but not for him. A lot of good was being accomplished with therapy. That was true. Still, he could see how the discipline was being misused. Theories of psychology, he thought, were often used to excuse personal responsibility for criminal acts.

Too often it seemed, the bad guys got away with crime because some other guy with a degree was able to convince a judge and Jury that the culprit was not responsible for his actions. In some cases, he was sure that was true, but it sure would seem to him that the discipline of social behavior was certainly being exploited for personal gain. So he would do the one thing he could do best. He quit the master's program.

Although Garry realized that by leaving college, he was technically still a quitter; he knew the main reason he became so disinterested in the application of modern psychology was what he believed to be the purposeful rejection by so many scholars of the spiritual realm.

He would never stop believing in a spiritual existence. It just made so much sense to him that the sure way to remain stuck in inappropriate behavior was to conform to this world. He would always be grateful that he didn't quit football and returned to practice the following Monday.

As Garry attempted to explain his thoughts to Barb, he realized his mind had many times transcended time and space. "Have I lost you in all this,?" he asked.

"Not at all, I'm aware of your beliefs, but I would be nice to get back to the game."

"Well, alright then." Garry responded with a fake frown.

Chapter Seven

No Free Ride

Garry knew even as he was returning to the huddle after Randy's first run, he was in a struggle with spiritual forces. The team gathered in front of him, facing the defensive team. He was always quick to congratulate any teammate who did well, but not this time. He was doing too good of a job conforming to the world.

Randy looked at him without expression. But Garry knew, that Randy knew, that the team knew, he did very well on that last run up the middle. Garry had only known Randy for a short time and talked to him only on a couple of occasions. It was enough to know that Randy had a tough experience growing up and going to school. "So what?" Garry thought. "My family was poor too. There were five boys in my family and my Dad only had a 2nd grade education."

Garry spoke to Randy shortly after he had transferred from his old school and had to admit that he was aware of some of his hardships, Randy's life must have been considerably more difficult. Randy told him about having a two hour ride each morning and evening on the bus to get to his old school. Randy mentioned other hardships, but Garry paid little attention. He had his own problems to deal with.

Standing in the huddle preparing to call the next play, Garry said to himself, "Yeah, that's tough, but I didn't get a free ride to play football and just because you had certain qualities didn't mean you were going to get a free ride either. I had a lousy three years of football. This was my senior year and right now I am quarterback."

"T40 on 2. T40 on 2." It was the same play Randy had just run, but no one questioned it. The team knew the only pass Garry was sure to complete was a jump pass to the right end. Jim, the right end would run a couple yards into the defensive secondary, cut quickly left and Garry would hit him with a little jump pass over the line. "Before I'm through tonight," Garry thought, "Randy will either be a hero or wish I had thrown a lot of jump passes to Jim."

In the last four years, Coach Hank had only said three complimentary things to Garry. The first was a couple of weeks earlier, after the team had beaten a rival team for the first time in seventeen years.

He said, "Guy-ri, you have been a pleasant surprise to me." The second was before the second game of the season. He said, "Guy-ri, it looks like you may have to be our work horse." The third was when he told Jimbo and a couple of other senior players that he thought Garry would be an excellent football coach.

During the season of his junior year, the team lost nine out of ten games. His team would also lose the first game of his senior year. But that game was much more than a loss.

The first team quarterback, Billy, twisted his knee and it looked bad. The following week, during practice, Jerry, the 2nd string quarterback, twisted his knee. Billy was a senior and had played quarterback for four years. Garry thought he was very good. Jerry was a junior and was experiencing his first year at quarterback, but appeared to be coming along well. The team was in a tough spot.

Coach Hank remembered that during the last three weeks of Garry's junior year, the team had lost some players for different reasons. There were just enough to make two teams for a scrimmage. His assistant, Coach Frank-the team had a Hank and a Frank for coaches-was choosing players from the second team to run offense against the first team.

Coach Hank chose every position except one. That one was the quarterback. He looked around and Garry was the only one left. He laughed and pointed at Garry and saying, "Hey Y.A. looks like you're the quarterback." The rest of the team laughed as well.

The reference to Y.A. Tittle had to have been his age, but Y.A. Tittle was a player Garry truly admired. Tittle played seventeen years as quarterback, and was called "the aging warrior." That reference didn't concern Garry in the least. He was also not the least bit concerned about playing quarterback. That had been his dream.

During that practice session as a last resort choice for quarterback, Garry actually did well and could see that Coach Hank was paying attention, though he said nothing. Garry had three years of watching from the sidelines. He knew every offensive play, but his experience came not from the team he was now on, but from playing neighborhood football.

Garry had organized a team with the boys in his neighborhood and talked kids from two other neighborhoods into forming teams so they could play against each other on Saturdays. They played nearly every Saturday. Garry always played quarterback.

His team never lost a game. He also played everyday with his next-door neighbor who was a year older and actually a skilful player. Garry had developed pretty good quarterbacking skills away from high school.

Coach Frank chose Garry to start the first game of his senior year, as defensive safety. When he was advising Garry of the starting position, Coach Frank only said, "I know you can do this. You will be the last resort on defense. Just don't let anybody get behind you." The team lost that first game 12 to 0, but no one ever got past him assuring his place as a defensive starter.

Losing the first game of the season was not the most serious problem. Everyone seemed to have the fear that the team would become demoralized, believing they were in for another losing season. To make matters worse, both the first and second string quarterback had been injured.

On Monday before the second game, Coach Hank caught Garry in the hallway during class change and said, "Guy-ri, I don't know if Billy or Jerry will be able to play Friday night. We may have to start you at quarterback." Garry just said, "OK Coach."

The demons were talking to him. "Did you hear what he said? We may have to start you." The accents seemed to be on the words have and you. To Garry, that meant the coach was thinking the team was at the bottom of the barrel and he was the only apple left.

Garry knew he would play a lot during his senior year. He didn't realize just how much. During the second game of the season, Garry never came off the field. He played both offense and defense. The team won the game 21 to nothing.

Although Garry thought he performed well at quarterback, even with throwing just a few short passes, they were playing a team with much less experience. But the win gave the team the confidence it needed.

At the very next game, they would beat their rival team for the first time in 17 years and continue to have an 8-3-1 season, including a win in their Bowl Game. They would end the season with the school's best record; a record the team held for many years.

But this was now. The season wasn't over. Garry still had this game to deal with. As the team returned to the line, He noticed the defense moved in a little tighter, appearing to have no concern at all about a pass. They were right. But Garry was sure the opposing team was still going to have all they bargained for and then some.

"Down!" Once again, the line and backs snapped into the ready position. Carl stretched over the football, grasping it with both hands. His back straightened as his head tilted up and his eyes focused forward as if staring down the defensive middle linebacker, who stood ready as well. With his knees slightly bent, the linebacker held his hands slightly above his waist and to both sides: his fists nervously opening and closing as if he was about to be overrun by a juggernaut. He was right.

"Hut one!" The offensive line and backs were like gargoyles frozen in time. The only movement came from the defensive players. Linemen shifted slightly and the linebackers pressed their cleats deeper into the turf for extra traction.

"Hut two!" Once again, Carl, the center, slapped the football firmly into Garry's hands as the familiar sounds of helmets, pads, grunts, and groans erupted from desperate players slamming into each other. One team pushed and clawed furiously to reach and stop the movement of the ball while the other team, with equal determination, put forth tremendous effort to clear a way for the one who was carrying the ball.

Although the play was an exact duplicate of the first, it made little difference. Randy smashed through the zero hole as if he had been called back on stage for an encore. His run seemed to take much longer than normal; probably because he was hit more times than normal.

A defensive lineman blocked the hole and hit Randy low as he barreled forward. A following action of being bulldozed by Randy presented an awkward view for the lineman. Now flat on his back, the lineman looked up at Randy's cleats passing over head. The next instant, the lineman's view was completely blocked as Carl and the middle linebacker came crashing down on him like freshly cut oaks covering most of his upper body and face. Randy was gone.

Randy, with his head and shoulders low, continued to plow forward. A defensive lineman got a hand on Randy's shoulder but lost his grip as he was being bulldozed out of the way by the right guard. Randy was hit hard on opposite sides by both defensive backs. Randy kept his feet for a couple more yards until the defensive end, like a bowling ball picking up a spare, sent them all sprawling to the ground. Randy had picked up five more yards and a first down. This was clearly no free ride.

Chapter Eight

The Tether

Then the mother of the sons of Zebedee came to Jesus with her sons, bowing down and making a request of Him. And He said to her, "What do you wish?" She said to Him, "Command that in Your kingdom these two sons of mine may sit one on Your right and one on Your left." But Jesus answered, "You do not know what you are asking. Are you able to drink the cup that I am about to drink?" They said to Him, "We are able."

"Just imagine," Mr. Andy said as he began another one of his Sunday School lessons that Garry was always so eager to hear, "the disciples were gathered around Jesus. They had seen what he could do. They wanted more than just to be a part of it. They wanted to be seated next to the master."

"How important is prominence to us as human beings?" Mr. Andy asked and answered his own question before anyone could respond. "Very important!" He said with emphasis. "A position of prominence was not only important to James and John. It was apparently very important to their mother since she was the one who approached Jesus with the request."

"Do you remember how Jesus responded to the concept of position?" Mr. Andy asked. Answering his own question again, he added, "He washed the feet of his disciples."

"Okay," Garry thought to himself. "I am a quarterback. Do I try to flaunt it. No! I know how I got here, and so does the rest of the team. I mean, I've never tried to be impressive. Just look at the one chance I had to make a touchdown in the first game I quarterbacked. We were two yards from the goal line. Carl tried to get me to run a quarterback sneak. It was a sure score! But did I do it? No, not me. I had to be humble and let someone else have the glory."

Garry remembered the Sunday school lesson about wanting glory that wasn't deserved. He believed he certainly didn't deserve any glory. Instead of making a touchdown himself as he had always dreamed of doing, he let George run the ball in for the score. "Wasn't that kind of like Jesus washing the apostles' feet? Surely I was being humble and doing the right thing." As Garry thought to himself, without realizing it, his attempt at being humble was his way of combating the demons.

The demons were fighting back with equal determination and appeared to be winning. "After all, I shouldn't make a touchdown. I was the slowest runner on the team. Even Jimbo, the tackle, had won a bet by out running me in a 100 yard sprint. His reward, like everything else associated with football, was humiliating. He got to kick my butt in front of other players."

Mr. Andy's words came with authority. "Now listen class. Proverbs 23:7 says, as a man thinks in his heart, so is he. Think about what you think about. Words are powerful. You will become the way you think! Like leaves falling from a tree, you only notice them as they strike against you or you see them. But leaves are leaves. Words are all together different. Words aren't things you can see or reach out and touch with your hand. But they are real and more powerful than you can imagine. Words can direct a person's life. Words can lead a country or a world to war or peace!"

Mr. Andy paused for a moment as he looked intently at each member of the class. The silence was a technique he often used to draw every eye toward him. His eyes would squint. His lips would tighten. An almost inaudible lengthy sigh would escape his lips-not as expressing disapproval by a teacher-more like a weight lifter preparing to set a record. "Think about," he would pause and sigh again, What you think about! When you accept Jesus Christ as your Lord and savior, you have not only assured yourself of a position in heaven, you have also enlisted in his army and you can be sure you are in a war!"

Mr. Andy sighed again, lowered his head, and speaking more softly. "The problem is many of you may not even realize you are in a war until you have suffered so much damage. It is the damage that you could have avoided if you had learned how to resist. The words that will control you will form thoughts and the thoughts will become strongholds in your mind."

Looking the class members over to see if he had their attention, Mr. Andy continued, "A thought can be like the wind bumping against a balloon that has broken free from its tether. It will move through the air with the wind until a breeze strikes it from a different direction. The balloon has no choice but to move with the wind. A person can choose to stand against the wind, or a person can choose to cling to that which it is tethered. Be very careful what you cling to."

It would be much later in life that Garry would truly appreciate what Mr. Andy had taught him. The lesson Garry was learning seemed to be that it didn't matter how much someone tried to do right or how hard he worked at something, some people were always going to be less than. In his mind, he was clearly the one who was less than. Like so many, he was slowly becoming a casualty of war.

Garry lifted the cup of coffee to his lips and looked toward the dancing flames in his fireplace. "How easy it is to become a fish that doesn't know it's wet." He thought to himself. He recalled many events throughout his life that demanded his complete attention. Each event became a separate chapter in a never ending book, transitioning to the next, as it introduced a new set of thoughts that would draw the mind in a different direction, leading him farther and farther away from the course he needed to travel. The enemy has powerful weapons in his arsenal, yet they are simple. They could be nothing more than deception and lies. But to a mind that is not tethered properly, the result will be the same. Like a balloon that is not tethered properly, it will become lost in the wind.

Chapter Nine

Why?

The team had moved the ball past the 30 yard line in two plays. It was first down. Not bad for two runs. Garry had to make a choice. Randy had done well on both plays, considering he was going up the middle. Garry had to decide whether to continue with coach Hank's instructions or give Randy a break?

Spiritual warfare is tough, especially if you don't know it's going on inside your mind. Coach Hank's focus was on the field, resembling a falcon perched above his prey. Garry expected him to send someone in to call another play, but it was clear as he returned to the huddle, Coach Hank had left the play calling to Garry. Randy's breathing had increased slightly. Garry thought Randy was watching him with the same intensity as Coach Hank.

The cheer leaders on both sides of the field were shouting something as an obvious encouragement to both teams. The sound of a car horn passing near the field competed with them. "How odd," Garry thought. "The guy in that car couldn't care less about what's happening on the field. He just wants to be noticed. The cheerleaders, the band members and even the folks in the stands had their own agenda." Garry tried to convince himself that the only thing that mattered was on the field and the fact he was supposed to give a rooky a chance that he himself never got.

Just like the balloon in the wind, how quickly the spiritual attacks change the direction of thought. Garry had already forgotten about the Sunday School lesson. His focus was back on himself. He would run Randy alright-back up the middle.

"T41 on two." He said, leaning to one side of the huddle and then the other. Randy looked down for a second, without saying anything. The rest of the team was equally silent. The play was a simple up the middle hand off, but this time on the left of the center. Since they were closer to the center of the field, Garry thought it would be a safe call.

The team jogged back to the line. "Down, Ready, Set, Hut one, hut two," Garry barked. This time, with the third snap of the ball, Randy came crashing through on Garry's left side. He received the ball cleanly, but an opponent hit him before he could get past the line of scrimmage. It didn't seem to matter. Randy wouldn't stop. Five yards later, someone finally brought him down.

Garry noticed Randy didn't bounce back to his feet as quickly as before. He took several hits before going down. Now breathing even harder, he was the last one to return to the huddle, but he had taken them from the twenty to the thirty five yard line in three runs. Garry looked at Randy and asked, "Are you up for it?" In a low tone, he only said, "Yeah."

"T42 on two." Garry called to each side of the huddle. It was almost the identical play, just one more position to the right of center. "If Randy could get us back closer to the center of the field," Garry thought, "we'll try something with a little more dazzle."

Garry was sure Randy might have thought he would let him rest a bit after that. He would have been wrong. The demons were winning the battle. Garry was still pouting over being told to show Randy off. His mind was still churning with thoughts. "I wonder if this is to show Randy's abilities as a running back or a statement the coach wants to make about the school."

Returning to the huddle, Randy no longer stood strong, straight, and eager. His hands were on his knees and he was breathing hard. The defensive team called for a time out. Garry knew that the opposing team coach had to be frustrated at the way Randy ran over his players.

As the defensive team gathered around their coach on the sideline, Garry could imagine what was being said to them. He found it to be a little comical as the coach became animated, raising his arms in disbelief and pointing his finger at different players. "What's wrong with you? He's just another player. Ya'll act like you're skeered." Are you gonna play football or go home and cry to your mamas cause you got your butts kicked?

Now, if they line up like that again, you know what they're gonna do. If that back gets that ball again, I wanna see every one of you on im! Ya'll understand me?"

Garry didn't have to imagine the team's answer. Their shouts echoed across the field to the other sideline as they shouted in unison, "Yes, coach! The team could hear their coach as well.

"Now get back out there and play football!" Again,

"Yes, coach!" filled the air.

A quick glance at his own sideline told Garry that Coach Hank was still leaving the calls to him. Garry had needed to make a decision about the next play. What should he do? They were nearing the fifty yard line. The other team was ready for a run. He was sure of that. This would be a time to change things. He looked at Randy, who was still breathing hard. His team was ready in the huddle.

Garry knew the right thing to do was to give Randy a break, but the spiritual warfare was once again building inside of him. As Garry watched Randy in the back of the huddle, he could feel his jaw tighten in response to the anger that had been festering in his mind since Coach Hank said, "Run Randy a lot." His ever changing thoughts carried him back to 1952 when he was only four years old.

A more than usual sultry and humid Saturday morning in June forced slow movement from the folks who had come in to town for their weekly shopping. Women were cheerfully greeting neighbors, with each one commenting on the other's recent acquisition of much needed apparel and other odds and ends as they met on the sidewalk in front of the small country stores that lined the square.

Even with the heat, the town was a beehive of activity as cars entered and departed the square from each of its four corners. A small grocery store about twenty feet wide and thirty feet long seemed always crowded with more men looking for an opportunity to get out of the heat and talk about coon dogs, politics and fishing than making purchases. This would be a typical Tennessee Saturday morning in the early 1950s.

The aroma of the store was a tangle of coffee beans, feed for stock, and a couple of farmers who came straight from the fields to the store, along with cigar and cigarette smoke that floated over and between the three rows of merchandise that ran the length of the store leaving little room for anyone to go in or out.

Two of the men were sipping on a "cole drank" they had retrieved from the Coca Cola ice box at the end of the counter. The screen door at the front of the store allowed its unique aroma to ride the warm breeze, when there was one, across the room and through the screen door at the rear of the store. Air-conditioned stores in the small town in 1952 were almost unheard of.

Although a four year old may find it difficult to reason why, he can be quite capable of wondering why. As Garry sipped on his "cole drank", a Nehi Grape, he noticed two people come to the back door and stop. The first thing he noticed, of course, was the fact that they were both black. Instead of coming in, they just stood at the door, looking in. The man was holding a piece of paper in his hand. Seeing black people in town was not unusual. Garry had seen them in the alley behind the store lots of times. He wondered why they didn't come in.

Sixty-three years later, he could still replay the scene in his mind. The couple stood at the door for what seemed like several minutes without knocking or calling to anyone.

One of the patrons removed a cigar from his mouth and called the store owner by name. When the owner looked up, the patron tilted his head toward the rear of the store.

Without saying a word, the owner walked to the rear door and opened it about halfway. The Blackman handed the owner the piece of paper he was holding. The owner still did not speak to the couple, but took the piece of paper, walked behind the counter and picked up a paper bag. He walked around the store filling the paper bag with assorted items and returned it to the man at the door. He took the man's money and walked back to the counter.

Throughout the transaction, the patrons of the store continued to talk about their coon dogs, President Eisenhower, and their crops. Garry was unaware that he was a witness to racism. He would witness it again a decade later in the mid 1960s at a place he would never have expected: in church.

In the early sixties, the civil rights movement had started a campaign to change the scene Garry had witnessed in the little country store. Even church members were making statements like, "Black people have their own churches, don't they? I'm not sure how it will be if whites and blacks start mixing. You know what that's gonna lead to."

As often was the case, Garry began a conversation with himself. "This kind of talk is coming from folks who call themselves Christians? Why? Did God favor one group of people over another? Of course not. But what about his chosen people, the Jews? There has to be an explanation. You'll learn one day." Like so many other things, he left it at that.

He would learn alright. He would learn a lot. He would learn a new term. It would be "reverse racism." He would often think how

ridiculous that term sounded. Racism is racism. Prejudice is often hidden by those who enjoyed playing victim while denying the fact that they themselves were actually racists. They could point a finger in a different direction. Time and time again he would ask, "What's next and why, why, why does it have to be this way?

Chapter Ten

Strongholds

Garry remembered the morning in 1959 when his 6th grade teacher walked into the classroom after an unexpected teacher's meeting. The teacher gave the class strict orders to remain in their seats and stay quiet while she was gone. Her pet student Kimberly, who was also the daughter of one of the other teachers was, asked to be class monitor. Kimberly accepted the responsibility with her usual straight back, head up, look at me pride. Everyone knew she would report any misconduct.

Mrs. Taylor returned after about twenty minutes. An expression of dissatisfaction was on her face. With tightened lips, she snapped, "From now on you'll have to sit in alphabetical order. You can no longer sit where you want." Starting at the left front student's desk, she placed everyone in order. Finally, after reseating everyone, she said, "It looks like next year we will have colored students. "We can't show any partiality, so this is how it's going to be and you might as well get used to it now."

To Garry, the expressions on all the other student's faces told the same story, "What's the big deal?" It wouldn't be until 1964 that integration became a reality at the school. Randy was one of the five or six students who would become the first black students to enroll in Garry's school.

To say the least, seeing black students walking the halls of the old school for the first time was different. For the first few days, there were some awkward moments between the black and white students. Every student made a conscious effort, under obvious stress, to avoid doing or saying anything that might be taken the wrong way. In a couple of weeks, it seemed everything was normal.

Randy transferred to the school during the last half of his sophomore year. Since Garry was a Junior, their paths rarely crossed. In fact, there were no black students above sophomore. It was on one of the rare occasions of passing that Garry's curiosity got the best of him. He was sure the integration process was quite an experience for Randy as well.

"So, how do you like it here?' Garry asked. He had only been this close and face to face with a black person one other time in his whole life. That was one Saturday morning when he was about five. An elderly black man known as Mose was always in town, walking from car to car selling peanuts. Garry remembered Mose walking up to their car parked outside the same little store where he had seen the black couple come to the back door and wait quietly for the clerk to take their order.

Garry couldn't take his eyes off Mose. Mose was the darkest person he had ever seen. "Yaw like have some dees peanuts?" Even at five years old, Garry noticed the difference in the speech. But it was the color that amazed him the most. Mose looked just like any other person. He just had darker skin. If Garry could have seen himself, he would probably have been embarrassed at the way he strained his eyes.

"Couldst I shake hands wits cha son?" Asked Mose as he reached through the car window toward Garry. Garry couldn't take his eyes off Mose's hand. The back of his hand was so dark, and the palm was much lighter. Garry looked at his own hand. It was the same color all the way around. "Shake hands with him Garry." His mother said with a "you better do it if you know what's good for you tone."

Garry's reached out his small hand. Mose gently took hold of Garry's hand and gave it a slight shake saying, "Goot to meetcha son." Garry remembered the hand felt like any other hand. "Guess yaw don't need no peanuts today does ye?" Mose asked Garry's mother. "Not today thank you." She said.

Garry was still looking at his own hand, first one side, then the other. As Mose walked away, Garry said loudly, "Mama, the black didn't come off on my hand!"

"Garry!" she quickly responded, "You hush up!" Garry didn't know what he had said that was so bad, but he would always remember Mose looking back as he walked away. The frown of disapproval was undeniable. Garry thought there might also have been a hint of sadness.

Garry couldn't help but think of Mose as he spoke with Randy. He was very dark as well, but always seemed to have a big smile on his face. Randy's teeth seemed almost unnatural, as the sharp white clashed with Randy's dark face. The white of Randy's eyes accented the dark brown irises. But for the normal clothing, Garry recalled the Johnny Weissmuller movies he had enjoyed so much and how Randy reminded him of the "natives." He also thought to himself, "I wonder how Randy sees me?

Answering Garry's question about how he liked the school, Randy said with a smile, "Whole bunch more than whur I wuz?

To be friendly and satisfy his curiosity, Garry Continued the conversation by asking, "What's the difference?"

"Whole lots," Randy responded. "I always had to get up about four thirty in the morning to catch the school bus. Then I had to ride it about forty miles to the school in the next county. That school only had one room, and we had four grades in it, nine through twelve, but we didn't have any eleven or twelfth graders."

Garry knew Randy's home was less than six miles from his own. He knew several black families lived close together on a road leading out of town. Garry thought of the name for which the road where Randy lived had always been called. Now he was conversing with a person near his own age who grew up along that road. Looking at Randy and knowing the degradation associated with the name of the road, Garry suddenly had a feeling of sadness.

"And whereas thou sawest iron mixed with miry clay, they shall mingle themselves with the seed of men: but they shall not cleave one to another as iron is not mixed with clay."

Mr. Andy was attempting to address biblically the integration that was becoming a reality in the small Tennessee town. "Try to stay with me." He said, "This is a difficult subject. As you all know, I grew up in the town just a few miles away, known for not having any black people in the town.

I can remember when I was just a boy. I guess it was about 1928 or 30. I'm not sure. I remember something that happened just outside of town that I'll never forget."

Mr. Andy clearly was not the same self assured man Garry had seen in front of the class so many times in the past. He often hesitated, as if trying to find the right words, tightening his lips and taking an unusually deep breath.

"I didn't see this happen, but I remember the older men talking about it. You see, there was a small neighborhood of black folks living just outside of town. Now our town back then only had maybe two hundred and fifty people and they were all white until the black families moved nearby. Well, some men decided they were going to run them all out."

"Maybe they read that scripture I just read to you. I'm not sure. But one man: I remember him well. He was the biggest man in town. Well, they chose him to stand at the front door of each house. I think there were only about three houses, but anyway, It was his job to hit every grown man right in the face that ran out of the house. He did it too. They said he would knock them right off the front porch. All, that is, except for one.

The man was really old and could hardly walk. He had trouble even with his cane. He looked at that old man and just couldn't hit 'im. I guess that meant he had some good in 'im. But that's not what's important."

"Now I want you to think about that," he continued. "These grown men were doing something that I just don't understand. All the families left that town, and till this day, not one black person has lived there.

Now I understand that verse I just read to you, but you know what, sometimes I think folks use parts of the bible as an excuse for their evil actions. Listen carefully to these verses."

"But after the faith is come, we are no longer under a schoolmaster, for ye are all the children of God by faith in Christ Jesus. For as many of you as have been baptized into Christ, have put on Christ. There is neither Jew nor Greek, there is neither slave nor free, there is neither male no female, for you are all one in Christ."

Mr. Andy paused for several seconds before continuing. "Now here's the thing. You see, life is complicated. Much more so than I could even begin to try to explain. Most of you are about to become teenagers, and life is going to become even more complicated than it is now. But don't you see how even grown-ups do some unbelievable things while all the time believing they're doing right?

Now listen to me closely. I believe the bible is God's instruction book, but there is a spiritual war going on. You need to be careful who you listen to. If you let one thought get planted in your mind and you cultivate it and hold on to it regardless of whether it is right or wrong, then that will be the direction your life will go." Garry learned that the statement would apply to far more than just race.

Although the bell was ringing for the class to end, Mr. Andy said, "I know it's time for the class to end, but I want to read one more verse to you and I want you to listen carefully. You've heard me read it before."

He opened his bible to 2nd Corinthians 10:4, "For the weapons of our warfare are not carnal, but mighty through God to the pulling down of strongholds. Casting down imaginations, and every high thing that sets itself against the knowledge of God, and bringing into captivity every thought to the obedience of Christ."

He closed his bible and looked at the class, sighed, took another deep breath and said, "Read that scripture this next week and think about strongholds. A stronghold is like a fortress the enemy is building in a country that is not his. He will continue to build strongholds until he can take over the country." Think about what it means to be one in Christ. Try to understand that even all who claim to be Christians may not be one in Christ because of the strongholds established in the mind by the enemy.

Now remember this. The thoughts you hold on to become strongholds for the enemy. Throughout your lives, Satan will try to establish strongholds in your mind. You must be able to recognize them and use the weapons that are mighty through God for pulling them down."

Chapter Eleven

The Inside Man

Since picking up the old yearbook, Garry's mind seemed to have been traveling through time as if he had been aboard an out of control time machine. His mind continued the journey as he remembered Mr. Andy's words.

"What is on the inside reveals what is on the outside. Do you reveal Jesus Christ everyday or do you reveal yourself? Do you have an inside man who wants to do things differently than what Jesus taught?"

"Humm, that was a good message way back then." Garry thought as he picked up the coffee Barb had refilled for him. But it's sure not that easy." His fingers circled his chest as he began to notice that familiar uneasiness that began deep within, slowly emerging from a small decibel of annoyance to a booming irritation that lasted until the small white pill placed beneath his tongue once again reduced the amplitude to a level of acceptance. "The inside man." Garry whispered to himself as his mind recalled an incident that occurred during his basic training in the Air Force.

Black kids becoming students at Garry's school was not the source of culture shock for him, as one might expect. It was the transition from the small country town in Tennessee to a member of the United States Armed Service. During his tour of duty in the armed services during the Viet Nam conflict, Garry would come to believe that the concept of racism which was usually associated with the treatment of whites toward blacks in the south, was a satanic plan to divide and conquer.

Racism, as defined, is a belief that a race of people has characteristics that distinguish it in such a way that it is either inferior or superior to another. Garry believed that the concept of racism was only a disguise for the real problem that was at the soul of each individual-selfish sin.

"You really hate this color don't you?" Garry peered into the eyes of the young black airman from New York who was tapping his left arm with his right hand. The young man had spent his entire life in the so called "inner city." The question revealed more than curiosity.

He, like Garry, had left his home for the first time and was experiencing difficulty adjusting not only to the unyielding demands of discipline in military basic training-the young black man found himself for the first time, in the presence of real white boys from the south.

Garry remembered how out of place he felt as he looked around the barracks at the other members of his unit. Twenty-five of the forty-five members were from New York. Only five were from the south. The other fifteen were from the northeast United States.

"Hey Po white trash. Do you have anything to say?" Benjamin, a somewhat rolly polly white guy from New Jersey, was addressing Walt, a white guy from Georgia who completed the stereotype of a Georgia farm boy.

His six foot three-inch frame rose from the cot where he had been sitting and listening to the conversation about prejudice. Like the serpent in the Garden of Eden, it was just a matter of time before racism slithered into position to take advantage of the moment. But it didn't come from Walt.

Walt's eyes were steadfast on Benjamin. Walt's feet moved apart as his hands came behind him. His body formed the parade rest position. Walt's posture presented his two hundred and twenty pound solid form as one that had tossed a lot of hay bales onto the back of a flatbed farm truck. The position of his hands at parade rest said he was not in an attack mode.

"Well." Walt's voice was a true southern born Georgia accent unlike the overdone attempt by actors in the movies and on TV pretending to be southern. The word well, came softly from his lips in two syllables with an equal accent on each.

"First off," Walt continued, "I'm gonna ask you not to call me that again. Second, it's like my Grandpa said, If you take an apple pie," Garry noticed a couple of the guys looking at each other grinning as the sound of the letter "i" was accented in the typical elongated southern form and failed to roll in the manner in which they were familiar.

Walt continued, "and a cow pile-that's manure in case you ain't never heard of a cow pile. Anyways, if you cover 'em both with the same color cloth, it won't take you long to figure out what's underneath. What's underneath is all that really matters in the long run.

So as I look at every one of ya'll, that's all I really keer about." There was silence in the barracks as some heads dropped. In the silence, Garry remembered the southern phrase, "Nuff said."

Garry smiled as he tilted his head back and closed his eyes. As if he was watching a movie, the image of the quiet barracks seemed to make a cross fade transition, placing him back on the field with Randy still at fullback. Garry's smile broadened as he remembered calling the next play.

"T43 on two. T43 on two." Once again, Garry could almost feel himself back on the field. The mixture of sounds from the band, shouts from cheer leaders on both sides, and individual shouts of encouragements from some of the die-hard fans known as cable hangers who never sat in the bleachers, but moved up and down the sidelines behind the cable that separated them from the playing field, seemed faint compared to the heavy breathing of his teammates as they prepared themselves for the next play.

Garry quickly scanned each of the ten players who stood in front of him, nodding their heads in confirmation of their understanding the call. Garry looked directly at Randy. "You got it?" he asked. Although Randy's breathing and somewhat stooped posture revealed the intensity of the last few plays, his eyes reflected the same determination as when he first ran onto the field and into the huddle.

Garry turned toward the left tackle, "Randy, don't let Randy run over you." The team, laughing out loud, must have taken the defensive team by surprise. Garry's glance to the side line caught some of the cable hangers looking at each other in confusion. Randy the full back and Randy the left tackle had the same first and last names. The teasing that both of them often received from their teammates had become an inside joke.

Their name was where the commonality ended. Randy, the black guy, could run a hundred yards almost five seconds faster than Randy, the white guy. But Randy, the white guy, could be a bulldozer for about three yards. "Just hit the hole I make for you cuz."

White Randy's remark brought even louder laughter from the huddle and probably more puzzlement to the defense and side lines. Obviously, the two Randys weren't cousins, but the remark reflected the relationship of each of the teammates.

"Okay, break!" Garry called, slapping his hands together as his teammates ran past him toward the line of scrimmage. Randy had brought the ball closer to the center of the field and to the fifty yard line. Garry quickly glanced at the defensive line up.

The opposing team had brought the corner linebackers closer to the line, and the center linebacker and two inside linebackers could almost touch their lineman.

"This looks like a goal line stand." Garry thought to himself as he jogged to his position behind the center. "This would be a great time for a pass. I'll bet coach Hank would even like for me to pass against this, but he told me to run Randy."

As his team formed the T formation once again, Garry noticed the defensive backs nudge closer toward the line of scrimmage. "They know what's coming." Garry thought. "They just don't know which side. I've never seen defensive backs so close. All I would need to do is call a power left Navy pass and I would have a touchdown for sure. But then, if I did that, they would know I was going to pass. So, let's see what we can do."

"Hut one!" Garry could tell that twenty two players were ready to rumble. Garry felt like he could read the minds of all twenty two. The eleven players on defense were ready to stop Randy from gaining any more yardage. They were embarrassed that one player had gained so much in so few plays. "Was it because Randy was black?" he wondered.

"Hut two!" Once again, Garry's voice was a prelude to a massive human collision. Randy shot forward on the snap toward the three hole between the left guard and tackle. His hands were perfect for the handoff. Garry shoved the football firmly into place. Garry faked a handoff to the right halfback as he ran wide behind Randy.

Garry continued to run wide to the left as well, unaware that White Randy was being double teamed by the middle and inside linebacker. Randy had run up against a wall.

Black Randy quickly rolled counter clockwise to his left and started toward the left side of the line. The right defensive linebacker had cut across to where he thought Randy was going, only to be taken out of the play by Jimbo, the right tackle. The defensive backs had also moved up.

Randy, still in the backfield, spun toward the line of scrimmage where he was met by the defensive end. Randy took the full hit and spun clockwise to break the tackle. He was hit immediately by the right defensive back. Randy struggled forward, gaining five yards before he was finally brought down.

After everyone else was back on their feet, the Referee called time out when he saw one of the defensive players still on the ground. Garry's team hustled back in place and took a knee. Each teammate congratulated Randy for his extra effort. Garry thought to himself, "It's all about the inside man."

Chapter Twelve

More Than You Can Bear

Garry's glance fell once again upon a reflection of over fifty years of personal history. It was the group picture of his old team. "How long ago that was," He said to himself. His eyes, like a slow zooming movie camera, closed in on rows of young boys standing proudly in their uniforms. The soothing flames of the fireplace flickered in rhythm, almost emulating the sound of a musical score as the first scene of a classic movie faded in.

Then came the abrupt and startling change as the music climaxed with one unnerving off key chord. The slow zoom immediately changed to supersonic speed and brought into full frame one particular individual. It was one that Garry did not want to comment on when he first opened his year book. Garry's time traveling mind sank into an abyss, only to emerge forty years in the past.

"Garry, I hate to be the one to bring you the bad news." The sentence exploded in his mind. The words, though already spoken, seemed to dangle in the form of chaotic visions in his mind. He thought he heard Barb ask what was wrong, but he was unsure of even that. He was sure he heard the words "bad news." Images of one or maybe both his parents being in an accident flashed through his mind. He knew his dad had been sick. Could he have been taken to the hospital? How bad was he?

"But your brother.....," Again came the images.

"It's Barry," he thought to himself. He's in trouble again. Could he be in jail? Why won't that boy straighten up?" The words continued,

"Just shot and killed....."

Garry's mind transitioned to other images and more sustained shock. "Oh no. Had he had been drinking again? Had he actually done this? Was it his wife? They have been having problems for a while."

Garry felt himself reeling from the aftershock of a massive explosion as the last word sank in.

"himself!" The phone fell from Garry's hand as he seemed to deflate into the sofa.

Garry was just finishing his Junior year in college. Everything was gong so well. He was chosen as an assistant pastor in his church. He had plans for what he would do after graduation. The last three years had left him feeling he was on top of the world. He was confident it was all because of his progress in his new church.

Becoming a member of that church was a giant step for Garry. It required him leaving the church he had grown up in and basically closing the book on Mr. Andy.

After leaving his childhood church and six years of searching, Garry had become convinced he had found the right church. It took him that long to overcome some strange concepts. But he believed he was being guided by the Spirit and would eventually pull down all the barriers and "strongholds in his mind" as they were called. How strange it would be that the very vessel he had boarded would lead to even more confusion that resulted in him leaving "church" altogether.

Garry had become convinced that even with so many friendly souls in the new church who were dedicated to God, there would be too many obstacles for him to overcome. The members seemed to worship a tradition they thought brought them closer to God than any other Christian group. While in their presence, Garry couldn't help but sense they had a misconception of being a part of the more blessed.

Garry wrestled with the same two word question that would torture countless people over the centuries: why me? This was a question that only developed into more questions. Why has God abandoned me? Where did I go wrong? Have I not tried to do the right things when so many around tried to influence me to do wrong? Didn't I pull myself out of an environment that should have led to nothing but failure? Is there a true church? Does God even hear prayers? If he really cared, would he let such things happen? How long does it take? What do you have to do? Is there really truth in anything?

Garry felt the gentle squeeze of Barb's hand on his shoulder. "I thought you were asleep." Barb said as she sat down beside him.

"No." Garry said, "I just noticed Barry in the team picture. That was his freshman year."

"You still think about him a lot don't you?" asked Barb.

"Just about every day." He replied.

"I wish there was something I could say or do." Barb said softly. Garry only nodded. He knew that such a loss was too personal for anyone to understand unless they had experienced it themselves. But for Garry, that phone call on a rainy afternoon in early April forty years earlier produced a dark cloud of confusion that would surround him and impede his Christian walk for the next thirty years.

His brother's death seemed to be a catalyst to a slow and almost unnoticeable descent in Garry's life. With only one semester to go in college, his grades were declining. He dropped out, thinking a change to steady employment was what he needed. He decided that psychology, the major he had chosen, had become to him like the church: just a product of someone else's opinion.

If there had been anything real about the education he was receiving, wouldn't he have been able to recognize his brother's symptoms? Especially since his mother had mentioned Barry appeared more troubled than usual. Shouldn't he have been able to help? After all, only two weeks prior to his brother's death, he had asked to borrow Garry's .22 pistol to do some target practice.

"Why didn't I see that?" Garry asked himself? Then he answered his own question. "Of course I couldn't see it. I was too much into me and all that I was going to accomplish. After all, I was the first in my family to even finish high school, and then, only to become a college dropout."

Then there was his church. Just like football, one case of failure and humiliation followed another. He had put everything into that church, but like everything else for Garry, something had been lacking. The more he learned about the church and its foundation, the more he questioned it. He even went to the church headquarters for answers. The answers never came.

Garry convinced himself they never came because facts are facts and no matter how you tried to alter them, they were still facts. In the case, for Garry at least, the facts outweighed claims to truth. Even with what seemed to be the best intentions, everything seemed to be only a mass of deception.

Only a year after Garry's brother's death, the bottom fell out completely when his pastor came to him in tears with a confession. The pastor had been embezzling money from the church tithing.

Upon hearing the news, Garry just looked at his friend in disbelief. How could something like that happen? This man had become what Garry believed to be a genuine friend and a staunch believer. What was God doing? It got worse.

An investigation was conducted by church authorities, and to Garry's dismay, he had become a suspect in the investigation. Garry learned later that the pastor's Uncle who was also a member of the church and a district representative of the church, had spread the rumor that Garry was involved and probably influenced the pastor.

Although the pastor did the right thing and took full responsibility for his actions, things never were the same again. Regardless of the efforts he made, Garry continued to find problems with the church that couldn't be reconciled. It seemed no matter how much he wanted to be part of a team, he would never be a player. It was just like his football years.

For the next couple of decades, Garry would have nine different jobs. In every job, he would reach a point of success and it would happen. Something would go wrong. It took 15 years after dropping out of college to finish his degree in psychology. Garry seemed to have traveled a long way down the slope of destruction. At one point, he almost gave up saying out loud to God, "I've done all I know to do. If you want me, you know where to find me!" Garry was trying to give up on God, but God was not giving up on him.

He needed a miracle, and the miracle never came. Just like with football, he thought he should keep hanging in there, even if he would never be an athlete, even if he never scored a touchdown, it would all be worth it some day. Garry seemed to be so much into his own lack of personal success for so many years that he sometimes couldn't see the "forest for the trees" as the saying goes. He was reminded of a story his present pastor of 14 years told him.

With all the disappointments Garry had experienced with religion over the years, there was something about Pastor Mike that seemed to stand out. Pastor Mike was several years Garry's junior, and had become almost as important in Garry's latter years as Mr. Andy was in his former years.

Although Pastor Mike was "Baptist from the top of his bald head to the soles of his feet," as he often said, he knew there was more to following Jesus than being part of a denomination. He himself had experienced troublesome times. The thing that gripped Garry so strongly about Pastor Mike was his total honesty about who he was and what he believed.

Pastor Mike once said, "Some people really get into miracles. Like Thomas in the New Testament, they just have to see for themselves. It reminds me of a story I once heard.

A river had flooded, almost destroying a small town that sat on its bank. Well, one little house washed clean off its foundation and floated away. An old man who lived alone was in the house as it floated away.

The old man was a strong, dedicated Baptist, much like me. Well, he crawled out a window and worked himself upon to the roof of his house. Seeing his predicament, he did the only logical thing. He started to pray, totally convinced that he needed a miracle. He was determined and would wait for God to save him.

After he had prayed for a couple of minutes, his house floated close to the bank where some men were standing with a long rope. One of them called to the old man and told him to grab the rope when it was thrown to him and tie it around his waist. That way, he could jump from the roof and be pulled safely to the shore.

The old man looked at the men on the bank of the river, then looked at the river that was moving along pretty fast, and decided he had a better idea. He told the men thanks, but he would continue praying because he knew God would save him. Well, not long after that, some men in a fishing boat came up to the side of the house as it continued to float down the river. Two men grabbed hold of the roof and told the old man to get in and they would take him to safety.

The old man looked at the boat and decided it was too full of people who had already been rescued and was afraid that if he got in, it might capsize. So, he told them no thanks because he was praying and he knew God would save him. The boat pulled away and a couple minutes later, the old man saw a part of the house break away.

He knew it was time to double down on his prayers. As he was praying, a helicopter flew up and was hovering overhead. The old man saw a cable with a kind of chair on the end of it being lowered from the helicopter.

The wind had already picked up and the wind from the rotor blades, along with the sloshing of the water on the side of the house, created a most uneasy situation for the old man. Then came the thundering blast of a voice from a speaker attached to the bottom of the helicopter.

"Get in the chair and buckle yourself in so we can pull you up. Your house won't last much longer in this wind and that rough current!" The old man looked at the chair swaying and circling around as it descended from the helicopter. He was sure he couldn't get in without falling into the river, so he waved the helicopter on. The pilot made a couple more futile pleas, then decided for his own safety and that of his crew, he had to fly away, leaving the old man on the roof.

Well, the old man raised both hands to the heavens and cried out in a very loud voice, "Lord, why have you left me in this predicament? Have I not been a good Baptist? Didn't I do everything I was supposed to do? I've attended church every Sunday and Wednesday. I have even taught Sunday School and now, being lost in this river is what I get? Then a gentle thought came to the old man saying, I offered you a rope, a boat, and a helicopter and you refused all of them."

Garry recalled a miracle he had witnessed himself. It involved his baby girl, who was in an accident with him when she was only seven months old. That was before seat belts and baby safety seats were law.

Garry's baby girl was lying in the seat next to him as he was returning from a brief trip to a convenient store. As he drove along, she lay in the seat next to him, kicking her little bare feet against his leg to get his attention. He took hold of her foot, gently squeezed and shook it and said, "Don't worry little button, I know you're there. A thunderous boom interrupted the smile on her face, followed by what seemed like a few seconds of darkness. Garry's head had hit the windshield, causing him to black out.

The next thing he remembered was leaning up against the side of his car with someone holding his baby girl. He had run a stop sign, and a car had struck the left front of his. Although groggy, Garry noticed an enormous lump on the side of his daughter's head.

Events following that were cloudy for Garry, but he remembered being told that his daughter had stopped breathing twice while being transported to the hospital. Her fractured skull would require surgery. The surgeon informed him that his baby girl would have to have a plate put in the side of her head, but it would be two more years before that could happen.

She would have to be guarded closely. He said it was also possible that she might not walk or talk. Many people prayed for his baby girl, including many in the church he would leave.

Barb had pulled a chair close to Garry and had leaned her head on his shoulder. He smiled and gave silent praise to God for his baby girl, who now had a baby girl of her own. Garry's smile broadened as he thought of the doctor's words. "She might not walk or talk." From the moment she spoke her first word and took her first step, she just got better and better at both!

Garry had seen a miracle and believed he would see another as he gently placed his finger above Barb's right brow, moved it around her eye and down the side of her face. Barb sighed as she always did as she felt the relaxing touch. Just behind her right eye was a devil she had been fighting for more than a decade. It had caused her to lose vision in that eye and continued to threaten her.

Barb differed from anyone Garry had ever met. Besides this invading monster, she had experienced tough times of her own in the past, but never complained and never-not once had she said something as irresponsible as, "God if you want me, you know where to find me." She believed with all her soul that God was everything. Garry praised God again because he had learned so much from her example.

She had taught him the lesson that was so elegantly expressed by C.S. Lewis in his book, "Mere Christianity" in which Lewis said:

"People often think of Christian morality as a kind of bargain in which God says, "If you keep a lot of rules, I'll reward you, and if you don't, I'll do the other thing." I do not think that is the best way of looking at it. I would much rather say that every time you make a choice, you are turning the central part of you, the part of you that chooses, into something a little different than it was before. And taking your life as a whole, with all your innumerable choices, all your life long, you are slowly turning this central thing either into a heavenly creature or into a hellish creature: either into a creature that is in harmony with God, and with other creatures, and with itself, or else into one that is in a state of war and hatred with God, and with its fellow creatures, and with itself. To be the one kind of creature is heaven: that is, it is joy and peace and knowledge and power. To be the other means madness, horror, idiocy, rage, impotence, and eternal loneliness. Each of us at each moment is progressing to the one state or the other."

So much had transpired over the years that had to have been lessons from God. They were lessons which Garry, like the man on the roof, overlooked as he thought only of himself and how much he had to bear.

Chapter Thirteen

The T45 Option

Garry didn't realize it at the time, but God had been teaching him: not what Garry could do, but what God could do. That included the T45 option.

Garry had just run T43, which was on the left side of the line. Randy had made quite a showing for his first time to run the ball. He had brought it from the twenty yard line to the fifty. The referee had placed the ball on the left hash mark. Garry quickly glanced at his teammates. They all looked fine except for one. Randy reminded him of an old saying about horses. "That hoss looks like he's been rode hard and put up wet."

Coach Hank had still not sent a play in. It was obvious he was still leaving the quarterbacking up to Garry. Garry felt pretty good about that. Garry thought to himself that he had really come a long way since the day he first tried out for the team.

He had been the smallest, slowest, and least athletic guy probably ever to play football for that high school team. Yet, there he was at quarterback. He was fulfilling a dream he had since he first saw a team practice.

But Garry was realistic. He knew how he had become quarterback. "But does that really matter?" he thought to himself. "After all, here I am. The coach said I would have to become the workhorse for the team." Like always, Garry's moment of self congratulation ended abruptly with a following thought.

"Yeah, but I'll never make a touchdown. Even when I had a chance, I turned it down because I didn't want to appear selfish. And besides, it wouldn't have really been me. That big old center would actually have made it possible for me. I couldn't have done it on my own."

Garry was certain this game would be another win and once again, he was a big part of it. He was sure the other team was feeling a lot of frustration by now. Garry was sure their coach had reminded them that a "black boy" was running over them.

"Well," Garry thought to himself. "I don't know that for sure, and Mr. Andy would chastise me for even thinking wrongly about someone. But it's true regardless of what they think." Garry chuckled to himself and said out loud, "and here he comes again."

Randy appeared to not be sharing Garry's enthusiasm. He had taken some pretty serious licks. His hands on his sides, and the slumped posture was telling the story.

"Maybe I've put him through enough." Garry thought as he called the huddle together. "I started all this off with the wrong attitude."

"Perhaps coach Hank wasn't trying to show the black parents that he wasn't prejudiced. Perhaps he wasn't trying to show the quarterback club that he might have an excellent runner for next season. Maybe he wasn't trying to rub it on the other team because they didn't have any black players. Maybe he just wanted to give Randy experience."

Garry had seen his team's response to Randy. They accepted him just like any other player. It wasn't all Randy who had just gained thirty yards. The team was pulling for him by putting everything they could into their blocks. Garry decided he was going to pull for Randy one more time. He looked Randy straight in the eye and asked, "You got it in you?" Randy didn't speak but nodded an absolute confirmation that he did.

"T45 option on two!" Again, there was nothing but acceptance of the call from the rest of the teammates. They had been running straight T formation and straight ahead against the other team. They were clearly willing to continue.

Garry glanced over his shoulder at the other team before breaking the huddle. The defense appeared to be expecting more of the same.

The defensive backs had even moved a little closer to the line of scrimmage.

Several possibilities ran through Garry's mind. He knew if Randy could break through the line, he could pick up three to five yards. He could give the next play to the left halfback, who could surely pick up a first down on an end run to the right. But the T45 option offered just what the name of the play indicated. There was an option.

Garry had run the play a few times in practice and felt very good about it. In fact, it was after running the play for the first time in practice that Garry got one of the few "Way to go Guy-ris." from coach Hank. After he thought about it for a second, it was the only one he had received from coach Hank.

The T45 option was also different from the rest of the T plays. A normal play would require the quarterback simply to hand off the football to the runner and run a typical fake pattern. But the option required him to run very close to the line of scrimmage right up to the number five hole with a good possibility of being taken down by a blitzing linebacker.

The quarterback would stop almost inside the five hole and wait for the fullback to approach. He would then plant his feet, stretch his arms toward the oncoming runner with the football grasped securely in his hands and wait for the runner to fold around the ball in a typical hand off.

That's where the similarity to other T plays would end. Instead of giving the runner the ball and running the usual fake pattern, the quarterback would immediately turn his head back toward the line of scrimmage, hoping he would not get hit before the fullback reached him.

For any defensive player, the reach would be a clear indication as to which back would be receiving the ball. In this case, it would be very clear that it would be Randy. Garry jogged back to the line of scrimmage to find the defense where he had expected. It was close and tight. They seemed to know what was coming.

"Down!" The command brought the expected results with what appeared to be even greater anticipation by the defense. "Set, Hut one!" Garry noticed the defensive middle linebacker glance to his left and then to his right. There had been no change in the offensive backs revealing which direction the play would go.

Since the ball was on the left hash mark, the most logical direction to run would be to the right. The middle linebacker held his position but the defensive back to Garry's right moved up and to his left to cover a potential end run.

"Hut two." Garry took the ball from the center as bodies collided. He made three quick steps to the left close to the line. At the designated spot, he reached the ball back toward Randy who was charging toward the hole that had now closed.

Randy wrapped his arms around the ball in the correct receiving position. But instead of grasping the ball, he kept his arms more relaxed as he waited for Garry's signal to take the ball. Garry's signal would be a hard push of the ball against Randy's body. But Garry waited until Randy was hit by a defensive lineman. Garry knew it was time to take the option. Instead of giving the ball to Randy, he pulled the ball away and ran around the left end.

Garry saw something he had never seen before. There was a wide open space between him and the goal line. It was a goal line that was still nearly fifty yards away. It was as if he had stepped off the planet and into heaven. He could hear cheers from the stands, or was it an angelic choir?

A flash of light exploded in Garry's eyes. Was it a heavenly star? No. It was flash bulb Billy the school photographer. Garry was actually being photographed running for a touchdown. Then he heard it.

The sound of giant hoof beats were closing from behind. Garry knew the corner linebacker must have realized what was happening. He was still twenty yards from the goal line. He could hear the pounding hoof beats gaining on him.

Less than two yards from the goal line, Garry felt the corner back's hand on top of his right shoulder pad. Garry lowered his head and dove as hard as he could, tucking his shoulder and rolling on the ground.

Garry rolled up on one knee and looked back in the direction he had come. There in front of him and to his right was the goal line. He had crossed it! In front of him, and on his knees, was the devil himself.

It was the corner back who had been chasing him. To Garry's left, he saw what he thought was the most beautiful sight he had seen in all his life. It was the referee with both arms stretched high over his head. Garry had scored. Garry looked back at the devil on his knees and tossed the football to the ground as he said out loud, "I finally made it!"

Garry looked again at the yearbook, but this time to the front where he had taped the picture flash bulb Billy had taken. His face turned into an enormous smile. It broadened even more as he thought of himself looking like the Cheshire Cat in "Alice and Wonderland." He didn't care. What a memory that was. Recalling those memories confirmed some things Garry had learned throughout his life.

Chapter Fourteen

The Connection

The calling: We will find in this life that we are attracted to some things that may seem impossible to achieve. Yet, if they are important enough to us to never give up on the dream, we can see them become a reality in our lives. But these callings are often distractions.

There is a greater calling. It is one that supersedes material and temporal desires. It also requires choice and dedication and the necessity to "endure to the end." The difficult thing to learn is that when this calling has priority, all earthly desires are pale in comparison.

But as long as we are in this life, there will be conflict between the two. One calling will lead to a heavenly place, and one will lead to a hellish place. We must choose. As with the T45 option, the correct choice for a successful outcome is imperative.

The authority: As long as we are in this life, we will be under the authority of others, but Jesus said without the will of the father, no one would have the authority over us. While we may be forced to follow the authority of others, God places no force on anyone to choose.

The lessons in following earthly authority are many. Choosing to follow properly established authority will keep us on the right track. But earthly authority is subject to corruption. Valuable accomplishments and benefits are possible through following earthly authority. Gaining the knowledge of supreme authority should be the goal. To follow His authority is the right choice.

Spiritual Warfare: This life will involve confrontations and conflict from others. The conflict will often require preparation, equipment, study, and determination in order to be victorious. There will be times when we must do as Jesus said, "He that hath no sword, let him sell his garment and buy one."

But it is in knowing that in our earthly conflict, "our struggle is not against flesh and blood, but against the rulers, against the authorities, against the powers of this dark world and against the spiritual forces of evil in the heavenly realms," and that only when we are prepared for that enemy will we be able to become victorious in this life.

It requires learning the significance of the Helmet of Salvation, the Breastplate of Righteousness, The Belt of Truth, the Shoes of Peace, the Shield of Faith, and the Sword of the Spirit. It requires transforming to a character of Love, Joy, Peace, Patients, Goodness, Gentleness, Faith, Meekness, and Temperance.

The Tether: In our journey through this life, we most often anchor ourselves to that which we believe is in our best interest. Usually, the choice is fueled by lust, greed, pride, or some other misgiving in which there is failure to recognize as false gods.

The wind and currents of thought move us constantly in different directions until we are lost in a maze of confusion. But to those who will never let go, the heart can be continually renewed by a gentle pull on the tether which is the gospel of Jesus Christ.

Why: It is but one word and a question that is often never answered. It is a starting point for unimaginable success or unbearable distress. It is one word that can be the seed for doubt, fear, selfishness and uncertainty that will eventually erode into failure, or a seed based on truth, faith, and steadfastness that will develop into victory. Jesus said that in this life we will have trouble, but don't fear, for he has overcome the world.

Strongholds: After the invading enemy moves clandestinely into foreign territory, slowly and methodically, he finds ways to become accepted as part of the norm. His method is not to immediately destroy and conquer. As he identifies weaknesses in the defense of his enemy, he builds for himself a stronghold. His desire is that the stronghold he builds will allow him to eventually control the mind and will of the territory he has invaded.

"He was a murderer from the beginning, and abode not in the truth for there is no truth in him. When he speaks a lie, he speaks of his own; for he is a liar and the father of it." John 8:44 Too often, a person becomes a believer of the lie that has been placed in his mind and remains sadly unaware that he can constantly renew his mind. He can pull down the strongholds and have victory over the enemy.

The Inside Man: While many relish temporal success, they are unaware that any accomplishment comes by the grace of God. But for them, it is only temporal. They are unaware of the force inside them urging them on. They are also unaware that, for so many, the force will not always be with them.

Ephesians 1: 13 contains a special word for those who are true followers of Jesus Christ: "In whom also after that ye believed, ye were sealed with the holy Spirit of promise." The Holy Spirit is the inside man. True followers of Jesus rely constantly on the inside man.

More Than You Can Bear: A statement often made is, "God will never give you more than you can bear." That declaratory is as difficult to explain as the interrogative "why." For many, that statement is believed to be false and that God may use extremes to allow the sufferer and perhaps observers to understand the necessity of turning to God. He may give you more than you think you can bear, but he will also give you a way out.

The T-45 option: It is only one play in a game that illustrates future possibilities regardless of past experiences. Choosing the right option will change everything.

Garry looked over to Barb, who was now asleep against his shoulder. Slowly, he closed the yearbook and gave it a small pat. He realized that his memories of the T45 option involved much more than his first and only touchdown. It was one of the first lessons God was trying to teach him.

He could almost hear the spirit whispering in his ear, "These things I have spoken to you that in me you might have peace. In this life you shall have tribulation. But be of good cheer. I have overcome the world." Garry imagined Jesus saying to him, "Remember that corner linebacker? The devil will be right behind you all the way to heaven's door. He will do all he can to put his hand on you and stop you. Abide in me and press forward."

Chapter Fifteen

The Final Option

Ten years had now passed since Garry sat in front of the flickering fireplace reminiscing over his high school yearbook and sharing important chapters of his life with the one who had been his soul mate for the forty-plus years.

The smell of fresh coffee was still present. The fireplace with its rhythmic illumination still projected warmth. But instead of the yearbook, Garry was holding his bible and pondering the words of Eleanor Roosevelt.

"You know, I don't think it would be any more unusual for me to show up in another life than showing up in this one."

Many thoughts were cascading through Garry's mind. As if he had been watching a movie that was in fast forward, the thoughts raced through his mind, twisting, turning, colliding, fading in and out from day to day and year to year, reminding him of what was and now is. The reality of now was almost overbearing. Something was missing. It was Barb.

After battling for twenty years, she had finally lost the battle. Even with the years of surgery, treatments and countless prayers, she was gone. The house was quiet. The sound of hymns no longer could be heard from the kitchen. Garry closed his eyes and said with a whisper. "I don't want to think anymore." But the thoughts wouldn't stop.

"These things I have spoken to you that in me you might have peace. In this life, you shall have tribulation. But be of good cheer. I have overcome the world."

"What good is that doing me now?" Garry wasn't sure if he was talking to himself or to God. "Abide in me and press forward." Garry asked again, "Press forward for what?"

Garry believed the statement by Eleanor Roosevelt, along with other quotes she has reportedly made concerning the after live, revealed her lack of certainty of an afterlife. The quote also seemed to coincide with the beliefs of many others who inhabit the planet. "No one really knows." That last thought caused Garry to sit up straight in his chair. Another thought quickly followed.

"How in the world could you think something like that with all you have been through? Abide in me and press forward." With that thought, Garry smiled and relaxed.

He recalled the time while he was in the Air Force stationed in Northern Thailand. Garry was only twenty-two at the time and had become friends with a Master Sergeant who was nearing retirement. The Sergeant was a leader in the church Garry was exploring. A small group of about twenty people attended the church. Garry quickly noticed they were a tight-knit group and very dedicated to what they believe.

Garry accepted an invitation from a friend he had met when he first arrived at the Base to attend a meeting with the group. The church leader's name was Phil. He was a good example of what Garry and other young men in the service referred to as a lifer. Those who make a career out of the military received the title.

Phil was an excellent example of most career military men, with one distinct exception. His faith was always first. Phil would probably appear to most as a true GI Joe, but his strong military demeanor seemed to take on a unique transformation as he spoke of his belief in God. Garry saw the transformation as he listened to Phil tell about his prayer. Phil's story helped Garry to understand the difference between knowing and believing.

"You know." Phil said. "As I was walking along the shore of the Gulf of Siam one evening, I scanned the stars that were becoming more and more prominent against a darkening sky as the sun descended behind the waters of a calm evening sea. I was right here in Thailand on my first tour. Truly concerned, I felt like the Lord was calling me to follow Him. I was a believer back then, but I didn't know what to do.

I had met so many people in the service from different religious backgrounds. I faced every temptation you could imagine. Although I considered myself a Christian, I didn't know who to listen to. I found truly dedicated believers in all I had talked to.

So right there on that beach, I decided that the only way I could get a genuine answer was from God Himself. Everybody told me He knows how you feel and think anyway. I looked right up at those stars over the gulf and I told God that I was sure he was all knowing and all powerful and if he wanted me to know the truth, what he needed to do for me was so simple. Just rearrange a few stars so they spell the word yes. Then I'll know. You know what? I never saw the first star move.

Of course I was terribly disappointed. I wanted to know the truth. I didn't just want to believe because all religious people believe something and they have such different ideas about what is right. But I learned something very important as time went by."

As Phil was telling the story, he had been looking away from Garry. It was as if he was reliving the event in his mind. He turned to Garry, looking him directly in the eye as if to say pay attention now. Phil began speaking in a lower and more serious tone. "As you look back over your life, and recall passing events, you will one day wonder what your life is all about."

"I used to do that." He said. "I would hear so many people say they knew God spoke to them. I would ask them how they knew. Some just said they felt it. Others would actually say they would hear a voice." Phil took a deep breath and exhaled slowly. "You know." He said with a slight pause. "I experienced none of that."

"For me," He continued. I thought you had to actually witness something to believe it. You know, like the Apostles who actually saw Jesus after his resurrection. I mean, if you're a witness in court, you can't testify to what someone else has seen. They call what someone else sees direct evidence and you don't have it. If you repeat what someone else has said, it's called hearsay."

Phil looked away again with a sigh of frustration on his face. "So what could I do?" He asked, as if he was looking at someone else. "If I was going to follow Jesus, I thought I needed to talk about what I believed. Then it hit me. I realized I didn't actually know God existed, or the Bible was true. So I asked myself why I believed it."

He turned back to Garry with a smile and said, "Well, it's the same reason someone can testify in court without being a witness to an actual event. They are the ones who have been diligent enough to gather enough evidence that is reasonable to accept as true."

The corners of Phil's mouth extended, revealing his personal satisfaction at what he was saying and believed. "As a follower of Jesus, I have found that by actually being diligent in my studying and practice of the Bible, I have discovered a peace that surpasses all understanding. I'll admit it's difficult trying to explain that to someone else, but I'm sure that if anyone has the commitment and discipline to learn, with time, they will understand."

"Take time to learn. Be diligent. Be committed. Be disciplined. Don't give up. Endure till the end. Things are going to happen to you throughout your life that will cause you to become discouraged and question." Phil's eyes turned to a slight squint as he said, "Don't give up. God said he put before you life or death. Well, choose! You can either give it up or take the ball and run with it."

Phil didn't realize it when he told Garry the story so many years earlier, but he was describing the T45 option. Garry smiled at that thought. He rested his head back against the recliner. This time, his thoughts were different.

He imagined that one day he would cross that goal line again and it would be Jesus who would have both arms up in the air to say Garry had just scored the most important touch down of all. Satan was on his knees behind him and Barb, who had always been his greatest cheerleader would be waiting with a beaming smile beyond the goal posts.

www.ingramcontent.com/pod-product-compliance
Lightning Source LLC
Chambersburg PA
CBHW061357160726
47995CB00001B/355